Taking Liberties

Early American Women's Magazines and Their Readers

Amy Beth Aronson

PRAEGER

Westport, Connecticut
London

Library of Congress Cataloging-in-Publication Data

Aronson, Amy.
    Taking liberties : early American women's magazines and their readers / Amy Beth Aronson.
      p. cm.
    Includes bibliographical references.
    ISBN 0–275–97523–1 (alk. paper)
    1. Women's periodicals, American—History. I. Title.
    PN4879.A76   2002
    051'.082—dc21   2002022467

British Library Cataloguing in Publication Data is available.

Library of Congress Catalog Card Number: 2002022467
ISBN: 0–275–97523–1

First published in 2002

Praeger Publishers, 88 Post Road West, Westport, CT 06881
An imprint of Greenwood Publishing Group, Inc.
www.praeger.com

Printed in the United States of America

The paper used in this book complies with the
Permanent Paper Standard issued by the National
Information Standards Organization (Z39.48–1984).

10 9 8 7 6 5 4 3 2 1

For Nancy,
Who taught me what a woman can do,
despite the forces arrayed against her

Contents

Acknowledgments

It feels good to finally have the opportunity to thank the people who made this book possible.

My first debt is to my advisers, Robert Ferguson, who directed this project as a dissertation, Priscilla Wald, and Maggie Sale. Their input kept me going. I would also like to thank Beth Bailey for her help, and Lisa Gordis, who read my dissertation with great care and caring and who continued to support my work after I received my degree.

I am deeply indebted to several people who never seemed to tire of my travails or my project—or at least, they never let me know it. I am grateful to Amy Russell, Tamar Datan, Josh Gamson, Celeste Mitchell, Kathryn Glass, and Michael Sheran for their love.

I would like to thank Robert Aronson and Walter Robinson for coming through for me when I needed it.

I would like to thank Joy Harris and Bob Tavetian for all they taught me.

I am forever thankful to my mother, Winnie Aronson, and my sister, Nancy Aronson, who have never lost faith in me, no matter what.

And I thank my stars for Michael, who makes every dream seem possible.

A Note on Sources

Readers should be advised that titles of the early American women's magazines considered here varied frequently, sometimes issue to issue. Most often, variations occurred with the use of possessives and plurals. Typical shifts include "Ladies" and "Ladies'" and "Lady's." In citations, I have used the title that appeared on the issue from which a given selection was drawn. But please note that periodical indexes as well as other scholars have used other methods; as a result, slightly different titles for the same magazines appear in the scholarly literatures. To assist future researchers, I have tried to include both publication dates and the names of printer-publishers in the main text or the notes.

INTRODUCTION

I Want My *Mademoiselle*: Guilt, Pleasure, and the Politics of Participation in the American Women's Magazine

Ask almost any self-respecting middle-class woman in America if she reads women's magazines and she's likely to answer furtively, whispering, "Yes— but don't tell anyone." In a class or in public, these same women are likely to shout down the genre contemptuously, characterizing the women's magazine as destructively insipid, exploitively consumerist, and/or dangerously self-hating for readers. Yet the reality is that an astonishing tens of millions of middle-class women with much better things to do have been relishing a monthly *Cosmo* or *Ladies' Home Journal* for years.[1] Women's magazine readers are legendary for their loyalty as subscribers and participation as readers, even while they tend to keep their reasons hushed up or hidden. For many of them, reading women's magazines is a guilty pleasure.

Both guilt and pleasure have always been in some ways connected to the American women's magazine. In fact, this emotional mix was crucial to its history. From the start, women's magazines promised reader gratification, an offer indecorous enough to oblige shame-faced producers to conceal it in Early Republican culture.

But that cover, it turned out, is what made the American women's magazine the culturally significant publication it soon became. The first American women's magazine was published at the launch of the new nation, in Philadelphia, in 1792. As an inventive genre containing content deemed off-limits to a lady, the magazines had to attest to their noble character and high caliber. To survive and sell, they came elaborately draped in democratic dress. Like their numerous successors soon to follow, early women's magazines fended off accusations of indecency by their elaborate wrapping in the banner of democracy.

Many women believed the hype. And since the American magazine form carried strong ties to preeminent democratic ideas, perhaps they had good reason. In any case, the American women's magazine gained a genuine identity as both a sign and a site of a democratizing culture. Its formal qualities and public image together made it the place where women first came to constitute themselves as a distinct public in American life and letters.

As a marketing hook as well as a national ideal, "democracy" was certainly a winner. By the 1820s, women's magazines appeared in virtually every city or town large enough to have a printing press, cropping up in New England, the mid-Atlantic, the South, and the emergent West almost as fast as one can say "Helen Gurley Brown." Between 1790 and 1830, 24 women's magazines appeared in Philadelphia alone; 20 in New York; 38 in New England; 14 in the South; and 16 in the Western territories.[2] Compare that with American magazine production overall: in 1800, about 12 magazines were in print; by 1810, the figure was up to 40; and by 1825, there were just more than 100 magazines total in the young country.[3]

Women's magazines soon became—and have ever since maintained—a leading position in the industry. By the 1830s to 1850, several had achieved the first form of best-seller status, reaching audiences across state lines, reaping consistent profits for their owners, making names for their writers and editors, and gaining substantial notice from the press and the general public.[4] From that time forward, American women's magazines innovated literary, typographic, and occupational structures that set new standards across the field.

Today, women's magazines continue this phenomenal popularity and profitability, despite consistent and at times dramatic changes in women's lives. The top sellers remain cash cows even within large magazine publishing conglomerates; the best of the bunch boast competitive numbers despite the modern media explosion, garnering advertising dollars and cultural influence in an increasingly fractured and frenetic society. As images and ideals have emerged and receded, as political, economic, and social conditions have radically changed, as literary fashions have come and gone, women's magazines have continued to offer something that women want. What is it so many readers have been getting out of women's magazines that keeps them coming back for more, despite everything, no matter what? What's the guilt, what's the pleasure, and what else is at play?

I begin with the guilt, which for many a white, middle-class woman reader—the demographic combination that has always characterized the women's magazine audience—is largely political. It probably stems from the scorching feminist critique of women's magazines mounted steadily since the early 1960s, coupled with a coalition critique of the genre's social-class and racial ideologies.

It was Betty Friedan who inaugurated popular feminist criticism of the contemporary women's magazine with her groundbreaking book *The Feminine Mystique* (1963). Friedan's "problem that has no name" is the silence that surrounds the "happy housewife heroine," a gendered—as well as racially exclusive and class-specific—construction of a weak, passive, vacuous woman who is dependent on her husband for happiness and status, who is devoid of ambition beyond mothering and home decoration, and who lacks a voice to express the emptiness, the incompleteness, of her gender-delimited life.[5] In Friedan's famous account, the central culprit in the construction and maintenance of the feminine mystique is the popular women's magazine: this "image of the American woman," she opens, was "presented and in part created by the large-circulation magazines."[6]

A long line of academic discussion about gender and the genre has echoed Friedan's basic take. In general, the dominant voice of modern scholarship has condemned the women's magazine for debilitating women, making them dependent on men (and on the magazines themselves), preventing self-realization, promoting self-denial, and creating the reader as little more than ornament, object, euphemism, maid, or mom machine. Most scholarship has seen the women's magazine as capable of perfect domination, and its popular women readers as phantasmagorically "feminine": passive, dependent, and witless in the extreme.[7]

Although gender stereotypes—both of "masculine" domination and exploitation and of "feminine" passivity and victimization—inform this vision of the women's magazine and its readers, these assumptions have not given rise to many contemporary challenges. Even in today's climate of postmodern critique, of reader-response work in the literary disciplines, and of audience-agency research in the burgeoning field of media studies, the image of a perfectly maniacal genre preying on helpless readers largely persists across the academy.

This dysfunctional dynamic has been seen as nearly timeless—or at least as old as the popular text itself. Barbara Welter, whose oft-cited article "The Cult of True Womanhood, 1820–1860" assumes a passive female reader of all forms of popular literary fare, sounds much like Friedan when she argues that "Woman . . . [as] presented by women's magazines . . . of the nineteenth century was a hostage of the home." Welter, like Friedan, describes woman's cultural entrapment in a single, debilitating self-image that has been prescribed for her by a single-minded culture and that she has imbibed unquestioningly because she presumably lacks the proclivity or perceptiveness to resist. Both critics see entrapment. Here's Welter: "The attributes by which a woman judged herself and was judged by her husband, her neighbors and society could be divided into four cardinal virtues—piety, purity, submissiveness and domesticity."[8] And here's Friedan: "This image—created by the women's magazines, by advertisements, television, movies, novels, columns and books by experts on marriage and the family, child psychology, sexual adjustment and by the popularizers of sociology and psycho-analysis . . . is young and frivolous, fluffy and feminine; passive; gaily content in a world of bedroom and kitchen, sex, babies and the home."[9]

Welter's study of gender to the 1850s and Friedan's of gender in the 1950s have formed the historical endpoints of a line of critique that cites the same offenses and effects for virtually every era in between. Scholarship in disciplines from literature, to history, to sociology, to media studies has largely concurred with the vision of women's magazines as single-minded villains and their popular audience as helpless victims. Take, for example, Gaye Tuchman's 1977 edited book, *Hearth and Home: Images of Women in the Mass Media,* an important and influential early collection of social science essays. Tuchman and her contributors almost uniformly concur with the premises of Friedan and Welter; the volume's central thesis is typified by the title of Tuchman's introduction, "The Symbolic Annihilation of Women by the Mass Media."

Tuchman's view of the medium and its audience follows from research by the sociologist Harold Lasswell published in 1948—research that reflects that moment's terror of propaganda, instilled by the experience of Nazi control in Europe then heightened for many by the incipient rise of commercial television in the United States. This idea of the all-encompassing power of all media was quite pervasive at the time,[10] and Tuchman was early in her application of such analysis to gender. Yet the broad transposition of such postwar thinking to the gender wars of the Second Wave painted mass murder and mainstream media with the same brush. Plus, it cast the media's presumed extraordinary powers as both pervasive and alarmingly trans-historical.[11] "Americans learn basic lessons about social life from the mass media," Tuchman argued, "much as hundreds of years ago illiterate peasants studied the carvings around the apse or the stained glass windows of medieval cathedrals." "The mass media," she continues, renders all readers or viewers equally "illiterate" and powerless, and then "transmit the social heritage from one generation to the next."[12]

Given the historical breadth and resounding ramifications of such analysis, it is not surprising that so much scholarship followed the same line. That same year, Kathryn Weibel also edited a collection on gender and popular culture, and it echoed that social vision. Her *Mirror, Mirror: Images of Women Reflected in Popular Culture* (1977) suggests by its allusive title that mass culture is a mythic, all-powerful evildoer that relentlessly menaces and seeks to destroy the innocent, young heroines—who in this case are all women readers and viewers.[13]

Five years later, Marjorie Ferguson assessed both British and American mass-market magazines in *Forever Feminine: Women's Magazines and the Cult of Femininity* (1983). Ferguson saw only greater power and precision in women's magazines' ability to dominate, debilitate, and control. "What makes women's magazines particularly interesting . . . is that their instructional and directional nostrums are concerned with more than the technology of knitting or contraception or cooking," she argues. "They tell women what to think and do about themselves, their lovers, husbands, parents, children, colleagues, neighbours or bosses. . . . Here is a very potent formula indeed," she concludes, "for steering female attitudes, behaviour and moving along a particular path of femininity."[14]

By the end of the decade, this view had become more analytically nuanced, but its basic framework remained relatively unchanged. Kathryn Shevelow's *Women and Print Culture: The Construction of Femininity in the Early Periodical* (1989) describes an expert woman trap, in which overt and covert mechanisms interlock to imprison women. Initially, Shevelow allows that "covert rhetoric lies outside the realm of authorial control." However, in the end, she says that covert rhetoric achieves "results [that] do . . . support the overt, consciously intended results, and are, in fact, inseparable from them."[15] So, although inherent textual dynamics and reader agencies open up room for resistance or alternative readings, these possibilities slam shut when we are talking about women readers of the early periodical.

And over the past decade, most scholarship has critiqued the women's magazine as nothing more or less than the double-barreled mouthpiece of masculine interests, of patriarchy and commercialism combined—and designed to "annihilate" women. Women's magazines are believed to have increased in sophistication over time, but their middle-class audiences— despite marketing demographics that show a high percentage of college attendance and employment outside the home—are not imagined to have progressed a bit. Naomi Wolf's best-selling *The Beauty Myth* (1991), for example, explicitly locates itself on a continuum with Friedan and (more subtly) with Welter. "When the Second Wave . . . took apart what women's magazines had portrayed as the 'romance,' 'science,' and 'adventure' of homemaking and suburban family life," she argues, "they temporarily failed . . . [as] . . . women walked out of their front doors in masses." So, she continues, "the fictions simply transformed themselves once more."[16]

Meanwhile, as feminist women's magazine readers (like me) have struggled to justify our enjoyment of the genre, other commentators have begun criticizing, too—but from the other end of the political spectrum. Right-wing women see the agendas of best-selling magazines as excessively progressive. The Media Research Center, a conservative watchdog group in Alexandria, Virginia, studied thirteen popular women's magazines over a twelve-month period and reported in late 1996 that all are "left-wing political weapon[s]" that "hammer home a pro-big government message and urge liberal activism."[17] Christina Hoff Sommers, writing in the *Washington Post*, accused best-selling titles, including *Redbook, Mademoiselle, Good Housekeeping,* and *Parenting,* of advancing "Ms.-information" that "gives the Democrats a clear advantage."[18] In the summer of 2001, a furor raged over advertisements in women's magazines about the availability of the "early option" abortion pill. Conservatives castigated the magazines that agreed to run the ad. And recent books such as Danielle Crittenden's *What Our Mothers Didn't Tell Us* (1999) and Wendy Shalit's *A Return to Modesty* (1999) ally the feminist movement with modern mass-market women's magazines and blame them equally for leading women away from hearth, family, home—their true pursuit of happiness.[19] As Crittenden writes,

The women who buy these magazines today have heeded their mothers' advice: *Do something with your life; don't depend on a man to take care of you; don't make the same mistakes I did. . . .* So they are the women who postponed marriage and childbirth to pursue their careers only to find themselves at thirty-five still single and baby-crazy, with no husband in sight. . . . They are the female partners at law firms who thought they'd made provisions for everything about their careers—except for that sudden, unexpected moment when they find their insides shredding the first day they return from maternity leave, having placed their infants in a stranger's arms."[20]

Although this right-wing condemnation has helped some of us feel better about our reading habits, it does point to a problem of image, identity, meaning, and interpretation of the American women's magazine that has persisted for a century and a half. When the first women's magazines began to grow profitable, a trend led by *Godey's Lady's Book* under Sarah

Hale in the 1830s, many a male writer and editor decried such success as a female takeover and makeover of an important American form.[21] Some early feminists at the time also began to critique the genre, a few even publicizing a distinction between the conservative "ladies" who they believed were popularizing women's magazines, and the progressive "women" they saw themselves to be.[22]

The antagonism so long elaborated around American women's magazines simultaneously from middle-class white women of the Left and the Right (and from men all over the place) makes the content qualities, functions, and implications of the genre that much more puzzling, more intriguing. Is it possible that such comparatively privileged women readers have been so stupid, or so brainwashed, or so thoroughly co-opted since the launch of this nation as to have been complicit by the millions in their own entrapment and debilitation? Is the pleasure part of the equation to be explained by some long-standing perversity, by some kind of sick enjoyment of self-sabotage? On the other hand, is it somehow possible that women's magazine readers have been secretly reveling in an oasis of progressive thinking, an island of liberalism that has been able to withstand the full force of patriarchy and capitalist self-interest, plus the recent erosion of women's right to choose, the stalling of women's salaries, and even the "postfeminist" crisis of consciousness that many mourned as the twentieth century closed?

Clearly, neither scenario can simply be the case. Something in our analysis has been missing; some parts of the picture have not yet been seen. And the origins of that untold part of the story is what this book aims to explore. By looking back at the historical rise of the women's magazine, its formal qualities, construction of audience, discursive and decoding practices, public image, and all the complex moves and positions these aspects of the genre demanded of women from the start, this book seeks to reveal some of the missing elements in modern assessments of the first and most successful form of women's popular culture in America.

The earliest women's magazines actually offer considerable insight into today's debates. And it is not because women's status or identity hasn't changed. Rather, the main reason is that the miscellaneous form and active reading practices of the magazine have not changed as much as we might expect in more than 200 years of production. And it is this format, and the reader agency, authority, and selectivity it encourages, that allows divergent readings to form—and hold water. In fact, this history will show that conservative and progressive gender constructs have always resided together in the pages of American women's magazines. The untold story, then as now, has to do with how these divergent discourses have competed, clashed, and even at times cooperated in highly instructive and constructive ways.

Cooperation among liberal and conservative discourse has actually been a commonplace occurrence in women's magazine history into contemporary times. Take Friedan's "happy housewife heroine," the central character in the story of the feminine mystique. Friedan's narrative, although a scathing attack on the "writers and editors in the media" who have "brainwashed" women into thinking that their "highest value" lies in fulfilling their femininity, actually depends heavily on the popular sentimental-domestic storyline, an arguably conservative mode.

Friedan's "woman" is orphaned by a culture that has erased her career-minded mothers of the 1940s, she is excluded from all manner of public and independent pursuit, and she is repeatedly mistreated by patriarchal cultural practices. She is tried by relentless forces of gender convention that arbitrarily delimit and punish her, forces over which she must triumph to achieve autonomy and self-actualization—feminist fulfillment. Friedan's narrative so nicely conforms to the sentimental-domestic blueprint outlined by Nina Baym in *Woman's Fiction: Popular Novels by and about Women, 1820–1870* (1978) that it urges reconsideration of the many ways in which popular stories can serve a range of political ends.[23] At the very least, Friedan's unwitting redeployment of the sentimental-domestic plot reopens what Ann Douglas has described as "the curious and confused battle" against the restrictions of the "feminine subculture" through the forms of the subculture itself.[24]

These and other forces have been missed, or vastly underestimated, in women's history from the start. This book responds to some of those gaps. An initial issue is that even the sheer numbers have been shaved—for the early magazines under consideration here, by something like 50 percent. In their summary work *The Magazine in America 1741–1990* (1991), the eminent journalism historians John Tebbel and Mary Ellen Zuckerman have written that "forty-five women's magazines had appeared by 1830."[25] Archival research and subsequent analysis suggests that these leading scholars have radically underestimated the field. By counting extant magazines and also reading them, by following on notices of new magazines announced in others, the number of women's magazines that actually appeared by 1830 comes to at least 110—that we know of.[26] Perhaps dozens more may have appeared and disappeared without a trace to date. Patricia Okker, in her 1995 book about Sarah Hale and the tradition of the nineteenth-century American women's magazine, has identified at least 600 women editors operating in periodical print and publishing through the nineteenth century.[27] Although not all of these women edited women's magazines, Okker's findings suggest that reappraisal beginning with knowledge of the numbers is in order and overdue.

But this reevaluation will focus mostly on the unrecognized importance of the magazine form and format itself. It is vital to develop a broader and deeper understanding of the magazine as a genre in its own right, with its own history, its own unique requirements and expectations of readers, its own contexts and capabilities for producing meanings. Up to now, both scholars and popular critics have treated the magazine either as a poor relation of the novel, the simpleton cousin of the sociological essay, or paternalist advice literature in drag. The magazine's identity, genealogy, and functions *as a form of its own* have never really been seen. Yet I will argue that the formal qualities and unique discursive practices of the American women's magazine explain a lot—and advance the discussion a lot more. First, they explain how the divergent readings of the genre by the Left and by the Right can both, to some degree, be persuasive. More important, they enable the multiple uses of the genre, uses that have been effective for a range of women and gender politics since the rise of the genre. Finally, they also underlie the remarkable and enduring profitability of the women's magazine, if in different ways over time.

In the United States, the magazine has always been a miscellaneous and polyvocal form, one capable of sustaining multiple genres and competing discourses in a single text—and therefore conflicting readings, images, identities, and interpretations as well. From its inception in 1741, the American magazine was designed to entertain divergent contents and contributors under one roof. In a 1788 letter to the magazine publisher Matthew Carey of Philadelphia, reprinted later that year in Noah Webster's *American Magazine* (1787–8), none other than President George Washington celebrated the multifunctionality of the form. He endorsed the American magazine as "such an easy vehicle of accessible knowledge as [to be] more happily calculated than any other to preserve the liberty, stimulate the industry and meliorate the morals of an enlightened and free people."[28] Washington's words were perhaps more telling than he knew. By conjoining Enlightenment belief in advancement through knowledge with awakening faith in elevation through spiritual effort, the father of our country captured the definitive and most broadly "democratic" quality of the American magazine: its capacity to sustain competing discourses "happily" within its pages. By also alluding to multiple engagements with audiences—here the magazine affects the key Early Republican virtues of liberty, industry, and morality—Washington positioned the American magazine as both the brainchild and the helpmate of the emergent democratic culture.

Although the idea of the American magazine may have come from British examples, including the essay papers *Tatler* (1709–11) and *Spectator* (1711–14), and the popular miscellany, the *Gentleman's Magazine* (begun 1731), the American version was distinctly keyed to the democratic culture in which it was produced and consumed. From the start, the American magazine was more inclusive, more multiple, more participatory than any of its British forebears. Britain's *Tatler* magazine had its "Isaac Bickerstaff" character, and the *Spectator* its "Mr. Spectator" persona, each of which worked to center commentary and organize contents. London's trend-setting *Gentleman's Magazine*, the forefather of all gender-marketed periodical miscellanies in English, comprised sequential entries linked through carefully composed editorial transitions.[29]

By contrast, American magazine producers frequently presented anonymous contributions of prose, poetry, letters, queries, and fragments—whatever material they could garner by hook or by crook—in little apparent order. Even early American periodicals noted for their use of the Addisonian essay presented them amidst a more eclectic array of other generic contributions than did their British kindred.[30] Magazines' various contributions were typically composed by amateur writers rather than community leaders or elders, or they were simply pirated from other sources by early printers who then made scant effort to prioritize them. In fact, the earliest magazine producers worked amidst strong incentives to absent themselves from the organization of meanings in their publications. For economic and political as well as more broadly cultural reasons, the American magazine broke with its English ancestors on the issue of meaning, management, and control.

The first American magazines were therefore marked by rather uncentered polyvocality and by discursive competition between adjacent items on the page. They were, in the terms of the late-formalist theorist M.M. Bakhtin, "dialogic."[31] Bakhtin conceptualized an emancipatory potential emerging from the "dialogism"—or dialogue among divergent discourses and genres—that he argued was compelled by the form of the novel. Bakhtin's concept of dialogism has been applied by some to mass communications, but never specifically to the magazine or particularly to the women's magazine.[32] Yet the American magazine possesses all the formal qualities and capacities that Bakhtin attributes to the novel—and then some. If the novel, as Bakhtin argues, promotes equality through its interpolation of diverse genres and discourses, then the magazine does so by design: the form operates visually as well as verbally and embraces both polygeneric contents and multiple authorship.

The emancipatory potential that Bakhtin theorizes for the novel is therefore magnified by the form and function of the American magazine. Early magazines promoted "dialogue," and on several levels; indeed, they depended on it. Not only did they allow competing discourses among contributions and within contributions, but magazines called on dialogue, on audience participation and reader response, to perpetuate their lives in print. As a result, American magazines sustained a democratic range and also promoted the dynamic exchange of the often conflicting ideas, norms, and beliefs of audiences.

Whatever the account books and record books reveal about the instability of Early Republican print and publishing,[33] from the very first American magazines succeeded at generating ideological and discursive commerce among contributions and contributors. And actually, this deep "dialogism" could be seen as a vehicle for their eventual marketplace success. In the days before marketing departments, rapid reproduction technologies, and other expert capabilities for niche-making and targeted promotion, sales success depended on providing a little something for everyone—an approach for which the American magazine was exquisitely suited from the start.

In functional terms, the "dialogism" inherent in the American magazine configured a kind of forum. Its miscellaneous form embraced multiple voices, and its participatory format entertained the ongoing exchange of views. Through this exchange, early magazines helped develop new discourse, and new directions for the old. As competing discourses played off each other, they provoked revision, rebuttal, continuation, and other forms of response, at times legibly, from subsequent contributors. This relatively free play of competing discourse stimulated innovations in language as well as larger cultural narratives over time. As communities of readers and writers together wrote, revoked, reinforced, and renovated contents, they collectively negotiated and authorized—and the magazines disseminated—new discourse for public use.

For women, such "democratic" participation and the prospect of discursive innovation promised virtually revolutionary possibilities. The "political nonexistence" of women, to use the magazinist Harriet Martineau's famous phrase, connotes an absence of legal status maintained by numerous factors, including a lack of access to the public realm and to language with which to represent oneself there. Although public discourse itself was being stretched and pressured by the democracy under formulation in the

Early Republic, even the most privileged American women lacked language for their self-representation. They lacked, that is, legitimated language to speak for themselves in the public space and in public terms. As Kenneth Cmeil has written, even as new "democratized standards of speech were rousing and inflecting public debate," women's voices, if heard, "were viewed not so much as uppity women claiming equality, but as the wives and daughters of offending men."[34]

The 100 or more women's magazines launched in the first decades of the American nation partook of democratizing conditions and extended them to women—albeit only directly to those with sufficient literacy, affluence, and cultural clout—for the first time. Through formal dynamics, discursive practices, and popular presence, these magazines created the first viable opportunities to subvert and redress the problem of women's silence in the public realm.

At least part of the pleasure of the women's magazine experience has always had to do with an invitation to participation and self-expression within the magazines—opportunities that even modern women still lack, especially in public arenas from politics, to the workplace, to the press. For early American women, magazines offered such liberties uniquely, when no other print form or public place did. The early women's magazine made available to all women theoretically—but to some influential women realistically—the opportunity to break through a gender-imposed silence in the public sphere. And since magazines proclaimed themselves to be both products and vehicles of "democracy," the expression, exchange, collaboration and consensus-building were seen in political and nationalistic terms by all concerned.

The rapid proliferation of women's magazines—which occurred without the impetus or influence of advertisers—suggests the extent of demand for women's expressive opportunities in public. The specific kinds of opportunities these many early magazines offered women—and the kinds of liberties contributors took when given half a chance—will form the central commentary of this book. The pleasures of self-expression, particularly in the defiance of silencing elsewhere, the boost in belonging to a community of equals, the satisfaction of feeling central as well as a part of something with influence and cultural impact—these factors, present from the start, may remain behind the phenomenal levels of reader involvement characteristic of women's magazines to this day.

Even today's mass-market magazines—the advertising-driven, big-circulation consumer periodicals pioneered in the 1880s and '90s—carry vestiges of this heritage. Modern American women's magazines have retained a sense of "democracy" first of all in the divergent viewpoints they

Introduction 13

still can—and do—offer to readers. Consider the fact that *The Feminine Mystique* itself was first serialized in *Mademoiselle* in 1962, then excerpted in *Ladies' Home Journal* and *McCall's* in 1963. Or pick up a recent *Glamour*, and confront an essay advocating that fertility treatments be covered by health insurance on the same page as a piece about the mission and leadership of Planned Parenthood. One might find an advertisement featuring a super-thin supermodel adjacent to editorial copy critical of the resurgence in diet pill use among women.[35]

Today's women's magazines also continue to offer readers a more active and participatory role than any other popular medium available except, perhaps, the Internet. They still make consistent appeals for reader contributions (although more often now in connection with specific contests or promotions than for publication as general editorial content), and they invite more feedback (and print the results), conduct more reader surveys, reserve more space for reader letters, and respond more readily to reader demands than most other magazines, and much more than other media with segment-based formats, such as radio and television.

This is not to say readers exercise the power they once did. They don't. But even though reader participation is narrow today compared with early periodicals, the involvement many women experience with their favorites, the inclusion and valuation they enjoy, and the sense of connection to community should not be hastily written off as false consciousness or co-optation. These dimensions have a long history and political resonance for women, and in this age of postmodernist and "postfeminist" remove, the engagement that millions of middle-class readers have been enjoying might well be instructive—or even pragmatically applicable—for American cultural politics once again.

Of course, not all women have been invited to join the party. However promising the democratic opportunities organized by early women's magazines were, not everyone had access to them. Far from it. Magazine "democracy" in America has always been delimited strongly by race and money.

One need only refer to the enforced illiteracy of slaves in America, and to the struggles among freedmen to attain even basic literacy skills, to know that magazine subscribers and contributors were almost exclusively white.[36] Pass-along reading practices do make it possible that some African American women—the Northern teachers and nurses, and the free blacks employed in households as domestic servants in the era covered here— may have read the early magazines or overheard them read to others. Nevertheless, the struggle of the African American presses beginning in the 1830s attests to the exclusionary pressure of illiteracy and poverty, even among free blacks, throughout the nineteenth century in the United States.[37] Lengthy and official testaments to authenticity in the prefaces of antebellum slave narratives also speak to the problematics of African American expression, literary authority, and audience during this time.

The issue of affluence, and the relative social position it conferred, is relevant in a number of respects. Although an identifiable middle class is thought to have been formulated in the early decades of the nineteenth century—many say with the help of evolving gender ideologies purveyed by novels and women's magazines[38]—an unequal distribution of wealth, not to mention ideas about that stratification, have always been with us in America. Early American magazines were quite expensive. A subscription to a late-eighteenth-century and early-nineteenth-century women's magazine hovered around $2.00–$2.50 per year, or roughly what a skilled craftsman might earn in two to three days in 1800. An unskilled laborer would earn enough for a magazine subscription in about four days.[39] (By way of comparison, the price of a novel ranged from $.75 to $1.50 at the time.[40]) Although pass-along and group reading mitigated somewhat the problem of quite high subscription prices, cost surely restricted access.

Plus, even though many population groups considered illiterate could read, they could not write.[41] Women were rarely fully educated in writing; only when their families could (and would) pay for private writing instruction did Early Republican women receive instruction comparable to that generally reserved for young men.[42] These factors helped inscribe additional social barriers to magazine participation. Although "class" pretensions may have enhanced appeal among literate women of lesser means, real social class disparities in educational opportunity, coupled with costs, must have delimited participation.

Finally, many women simply lacked access to social networks that made publishing possible. The "democracy" of the American women's magazine, then, has been circumscribed by cultural restraints such as racial prejudice, economic means, and social status—and by the levels of literacy and cultural clout that tend to reflect and reinforce those inequalities. A few contributions to early American women's magazines explicitly articulate the privileged status of their dominant readers and writers; racialist and classist assumptions are at times literally written in magazine contributions. Those articulations are only suggestive of the social assumptions silently structuring what could and could not be said in the period. (Such hegemonic limits, of course, are even more strategically understood and manipulated in women's magazines today, both mass-market magazines for white women and those targeted to black and Latina readers.[43])

Still, in the early magazines, such sentiments appear less often than one might think, given the relative privilege we must presume among subscribers and contributors. Perhaps racial exclusion went without saying. Some cultural pressures may have also proscribed the articulation of these social biases in women's magazines, including, perhaps, emergent nineteenth-century ideas of gender propriety and political remove.

Moreover, the formal diversity of the magazine, the novelty of presenting women's works to the public, and printers' practical need for copy early on, may also have vitiated somewhat the outward expression of such structuring factors. Printers, for their own reasons, and white readers and writers, for theirs, elaborated terms for women's magazine "community" that in some ways circumvented other exclusionary hierarchies. Producers' interest in expanding the subscription base, and readers' drive for self-expression, connection, and a modicum of control fostered magazine environments that tried to efface or accommodate discrepant status. Publishers and contributors alike shared an interest in welcoming any comers willing to participate.

The compromising effects of racial and socioeconomic presumption on magazine "democracy" cannot and will not be underestimated here. As Cathy Davidson has aptly written of David Paul Nord's work on Early Republican readers of *New-York Magazine*, "the implied reader of a text is not necessarily its actual reader and any theories based upon readers' responses must be apprised of that discrepancy."[44] Still, however delimited access to early women's magazine participation was, it must also be recalled that much of the greatest writing about human liberty ever produced is similarly afflicted with such limitations. This fact is certainly no excuse, but it cannot be ignored as a context: the very thinkers whose world-changing works underwrote the formal democracy that formulated the United States also excluded slaves and laborers, as well as women, when endowing natural or inalienable rights. Even so, the language of these writers proved pivotal to political work by those not originally included in their liberatory conceptions. Although the women's magazine was certainly delimited by the operation of powerful hegemonic beliefs, the genre still provided a viable space for rhetorical experimentation and self-representation, revealed new angles and points of view, and demonstrated women's inclusion to other women and the wider public. However partially and problematically, the privileged women who contributed to early magazines helped write the book on "Woman" in the early American public—and that opened a door to expanding participation in the years that followed.

The same critique of race and class privilege applies to many Second Wave activists, who, problematically, took the white, middle-class, heterosexual female subject as their dominant image and audience. Friedan, for her part, envisions "*the* image of woman" (italics mine) standing behind "a picture window, depositing [her] stationwagons full of children at school, . . . smiling as [she] runs her new electric waxer over the spotless kitchen floor, . . . and [keeping] her new washing machine and dryer running all day." Despite the unacknowledged vision of all women as home-owning, heterosexual suburbanites who seem (and, demographically, still are) predominantly white, Friedan's book began a movement because it broke an all-encompassing silence. It gave a language to the particular concerns of certain women, but those women were culturally persuasive enough to make a difference for us all. Like the very women's magazine tradition Friedan critiques, her book made visible a constituency and a set of issues that engendered voices and enabled new choices. More diverse groups of women subsequently came to alter but not abolish her feminist language, and today are speaking out in new versions of its very tongue to represent with increasing fullness the interests of American women.[45]

Yet there has been less progress on changing the limited idea of the popular woman reader. Neither Friedan nor her critics since the 1960s have made room for the possibility that the millions of far-flung readers of American women's magazines might be the capable agents of creativity, contrariety, resistance, or change. In 1972, William Henry Chafe suggested that Friedan exaggerated her case against women's magazines, but his argument turns on the contention that the "feminine mystique" is simply older than Friedan allowed—not more complex historically or more open to reader reconfiguration or rebuff.[46] Recently, Nancy Walker has written that

While the magazines by necessity tended to preserve the status quo in their editorial content and stances, they did not, as Betty Friedan claimed . . . consistently promote homemaking as the only path to female fulfillment. The magazines also regularly celebrated women's achievements outside the home, most obviously by publishing profiles of and interviews with well-known women, including film stars and other celebrities but also women who had made their mark in business, politics, and volunteer activities.[47]

Walker's important critique of the supposed single-mindedness of the magazine form, however, does not lead her to reconsider assumptions about the docile acceptance by women readers of whatever content magazines choose to carry.

Unfortunately, much reader research has so far missed or ignored the popular women's magazine reader for one reason or another. Some scholarship on women and reading practice presumes that reading for oneself—whether reading "against the text" or not—is the almost exclusive province of elite, educated readers, who, accordingly, decode mainly "high structures, and so depend on the male producer–female receiver or male reader–female listener model."[48] Other studies of women and reception have assessed patriarchal settings and meaning-making.[49] Still other historical scholarship on reading seeks to theorize the social functions of literacy rather than of reading practices in social context;[50] as such, these treatments generally do not address particularized questions of gender or difference. Some work in the field has focused tightly on women readers' relationships to particular sorts of texts, such as advertising or fiction, and do not discuss strategies that may be carried over—or specifically left behind—from one generic context to another.[51]

A significant body of scholarship on popular reading, particularly reading of women's magazines, accepts Stuart Hall's model of "preferred readings."[52] Hall argues that such texts put forward a "pattern of preferred options in line with the preferred institutional, political and ideological order."[53] Yet this model still presumes that popular readers lack the ability to actively engage in any conscious criticism, resistance, or rebellion—an assumption that seems tinged with gender and class biases. And, just as crucial, it ignores any possible collisions among institutional, political, and ideological designs.

The latter possibility is particularly relevant in the case of the miscellaneous magazine. In women's magazines, patriarchy and consumer capitalism are almost always assumed to work together hand in glove. Yet, the history of the women's magazine reveals that these prodigious forces can be—and have been—at odds. At the very origin of the mass-market magazine, women's titles were leaders in the marketing of the bicycle, a brand new commodity that promised unprecedented levels of independence, physicality, and adventure to women—and disturbed patriarchal powers from many quarters.[54] Dominant patriarchal discourse would have "preferred" that middle-class women, particularly the young, single women who fueled the bicycle craze, remain within the supervised confines of home. But commercial imperatives clearly "preferred" that they buy bikes and take to the road. It was up to women readers to resolve the conflict of interests, deciding which arguments were more compelling to them and why.

In this and many other cases of collision, women readers have exercised considerable agency and decisive authority—at least within the confines of the magazines' pages. As a result, the early history of the women's magazine gives ample reason to re-consider prevailing assumptions about their relative abilities and opportunities. Women's lesser access to formal education has generally resulted in an assumption of their greater power-lessness and intellectual timidity with texts. Yet popular women readers actually did receive an education in proper reading practices elsewhere. As we'll see, early women's magazine readers were specifically instructed in ways of reading by publishers trying to sell more copies and stay alive. Besides, reading a few snippets of the often sharp-witted and opinionated contributions to early American women's magazines makes it difficult to believe that these women were simply the passive dupes of anyone or anything. Just read the magazines—the retorts to conventional wisdom, the forays into new fields, the righteous outrage, the empathy, elegy, the sly or coy or clever claims—and a new image of the popular woman reader must begin to stir.

Janice Radway's influential *Reading the Romance: Women, Patriarchy and Popular Literature* (1985) is a particular touchstone here since the romance readers she studied have received criticism and pity for the same victim-ization presumed for women's magazine audiences. But Radway found that romance-novel devotees used their reading in a variety of self-affirming ways. They used the plotlines to validate their own expectations of inti-mate involvement—expectations that fly in the face of patriarchal con-structions—and they used the romance to reject, for a time, "feminine" duty within the home, claiming instead some personal time for "selfish" pleasures, such as tending to their own emotional needs, envisioning al-ternative identities for themselves and their partners, and exploring the qualities of their own desire.

Too few other thinkers, however, have considered the multiple uses of the act of reading. Fewer still have considered the heterogeneous experi-ences popular readers may make from a text, especially one as diverse and tailor-made for multiple, moody, and serial readings as American women's magazines. Take, for example, the May 1962 issue of *Mademoiselle*, which, incidentally, carried the Friedan excerpt "Feminine Fulfillment: Is This All?" That issue also carried more supportive features, including "Disturber of the Peace: Ayn Rand," and "15 Girls Who Correct Harvard Men"— right alongside the obsequious "Clothes Men Love" and the insipid "We Could Make Such Beautiful Mayonnaise Together."[55] A reader picking up the *Ladies' Home Journal* of winter 1963 would have encountered Friedan's "Have American Housewives Traded Brains for Brooms?" un-der the same roof as an article apparently oriented in the opposite direction: "Ten Ways to Keep a Husband—Young Profession: Housewife."[56] That issue of the *Journal* also carried a feature by Dr. Benjamin Spock exploring a companion issue to Friedan's concerns, "Should Mothers Work?" (The answer is yes—if that is what will make her happy, if she is careful with her child in the transition back to work, and if there is satisfactory child care.[57])

Readers of American women's magazines have always been asked to negotiate divergent copy like this from page to page, column to column, sidebar to box. They have always had to be versatile and engaged enough to reconcile, select, and create—as with any text, within certain limits, of course—to suit themselves. Today, just as in 1792, the magazine inherently demands a certain level of agency and initiative from popular readers—what is called "active" reading—which flies in the face of characterizations of their stuporous passivity. The creative experience of such reading, moreover, may also account for some of the reader pleasure and power probably long at play in women's magazine history.

This book will reveal that, from the start, early magazines set about the task of constructing the female audiences they needed: audiences willing and able to read for themselves. Even if inadvertently, early producers created women readers charged with the gendered responsibility to challenge any text's ability to seduce, pacify, or debase them. Promising to protect women's virtue from the dangers posed by romances and other popular fare of the Early Republican literary marketplace, articles on right reading instructed women to negotiate conscientiously, taking in texts in episodic stints punctuated by critical thinking about content. The "good woman" reader constructed by the early women's magazines was made to understand intimately where a text was taking her. In the very name of her femininity, she was charged with the responsibility *not* to be duped or led astray by anything she read. That such an engaged reader might also be prepared to shift from the role of reader to that of writer would only enhance the magazines' prospects for longevity and success.

Women's magazines have always wanted readers versatile and game enough to participate fully, to both read and write them. So many *McCall's* readers responded to *The Feminine Mystique* excerpt that Friedan wrote a subsequent article based on their input—which also, in characteristic women's magazine fashion, kept the conversation going.[58] The *Ladies' Home Journal* was so inundated with mail about their Friedan excerpt that the editors tagged the April 1963 letters page with the stunned phrase "and they are *still* coming." And *Journal* readers were anything but passive, weak-minded, or mired in tradition in their varied responses to

Friedan's ideas. Jean Fields of Albuquerque wrote that "I need to feel that I am an individual, so I thank the *Journal* for printing an article which, for a change, doesn't glorify the kitchen and woman's role in it." Mrs. C.K. McCadams of Greensboro, North Carolina, by contrast, wrote that "the article by Mrs. Friedan makes me mad. So I'm a nut because I am happy and satisfied staying at home being a mother to my child and a wife to my husband?" Elsie Schumacher of Hollywood, California, felt that "It just goes to show—nobody's ever satisfied! I'm an old bag of 37 who's been looking forward to a husband, children and a home, in that order. I'll gladly trade my situation for one of those poor, tired, bored housewives who have the world by the tail and don't know it." "It is one thing to decry the role of housewife because of the demands it makes," thought Mrs. Richard Konzas of Devils Lake, North Dakota, "and quite another to in-sinuate that anyone active in the role is an empty being, devoid of any recognizable intelligence." Grace Decker's response pursued a different angle. "The greatest tragedy of housewives is that too many are married to boys instead of men . . . the problem is not brooms: it is manhood," wrote a Waynesboro, Pennsylvania reader. Joyce Fienberg, from Anaheim, California, waxed philosophical:

I, too, have tried various activities including university studies at night. I've learned something: that *there is no answer*, not until your children are old enough to give you breathing room. There's nothing wrong with admitting you're fed up; but for now, I'm the woman my family demands that I be. Later, I'll seek out the gal who used to answer to my name. I wouldn't be surprised if she turns out to be warmer and wiser and much more ready for life than when she was a bride.[59]

These strong-minded letters, written at the very moment when a so-phisticated mass media had supposedly brainwashed and completely silenced women within the feminine mystique, attest to the hidden his-torical truth that readers have always been actively engaged in some dif-ficult negotiations with the ideas they confront in women's magazines, and have always found a place in magazine pages to air and share those re-sponses as well.

This kind of audience participation made possible some important bridges between popular text and social life. Of all the engagements po-tentially organized by the genre, women's collectivity is perhaps the most resonant for their social progress. In *Is There a Text in This Class?: The Authority of Interpretive Communities* (1980), Stanley Fish has written that communities of readers actively construct collective meanings based as much on their own social positioning as on the stories conveyed within the texts themselves.[60] Media scholar Michael Schudson has also written about the collectivizing potential of involvement with popular forms. He describes that a key characteristic of the mass media is that their "production becomes increasingly embedded in a network of interaction, negotiation and feedback over time," becoming "more collective than was earlier the case."[61] Taken together, these arguments suggest that women's involvement with the early magazines may have indeed helped organize some forms of collective consciousness, a possibility that seems supported by the demographic overlap and rhetorical consistency found in early women's magazines and women's social reform activism beginning in the early nineteenth century.

In *Democracy in America* (1835), Alexis de Tocqueville, perhaps the first critic of American popular culture, theorized the collectivizing potential of early American media in political terms. He argued that in democracy, in contradistinction to aristocracy, newspapers would facilitate "association," by which he meant social organization, solidarity, and group process.[62] Tocqueville linked the spread of newspapers with the spread of democracy, but he feared reader dependency on the medium for constructing and legitimating reality. He worried that citizens of democracy would believe *only* what they read, and, in essence, that they would not know what to think unless it was created or confirmed in newsprint.

The interactivity and audience agency compelled by the early American women's magazine capitalized on the democratic association Tocqueville predicted for newspapers while forestalling the onset of mass society he feared. By encouraging women's public expression and collective participation, publicizing it, and legitimating the entire process in both gendered and political terms, magazines did even more than enable women to constitute themselves as a public. They also did so while forestalling the passivity and dependence that invite groupthink—thus creating conditions to keep that public ever alive and growing. As media theorist John Fiske has argued, an analytical "emphasis on audience creativity" is "encouraging cultural democracy at work."[63] This book aims to contribute to that direction by bringing forward the more complicated women's magazine and more sophisticated popular reader that American women and history deserve.

NOTES

1. Given the long-standing practice of inflating readership figures by adding estimated "pass-along" readers, the total number of actual women's magazine readers is impossible to determine with certainty. However, circulation

figures published by the Magazine Publishers Association easily support a claim of tens of millions.

2. See Caroline John Garnsey, "Ladies Magazines to 1850: The Beginnings of an Industry," *Bulletin of the New York Public Library* 58 (1954), pp. 74–88. See also Bertha-Monica Stearns, "Before Godey's," *American Literature* 2 (1930), pp. 248–55.

3. Frank Luther Mott, *A History of American Magazines, Vol. 1: 1741–1850* (New York: D. Appleton and Company, 1930).

4. Ibid.

5. See Betty Friedan, *The Feminine Mystique* (New York: Dell Publishing, 1983), pp. 15–79.

6. Ibid., p. 34.

7. Indeed, extenuating from this view of women's magazine readers, millions of women viewers of "feminine" forms of mass media, most notably the soap opera, have been similarly assessed. Tanya Modleski's famous characterization of women soap opera fans as "egoless receptacles" has been quite widely argued or assumed about women's magazine readers as well. See Tanya Modleski, "The Search for Tomorrow in Today's Soap Operas," in *Loving with a Vengeance: Mass-Produced Fantasies for Women* (Hamden, CT: The Shoestring Press, 1982).

8. Barbara Welter, "The Cult of True Womanhood, 1820–1860," *American Quarterly*, vol. 18, no. 2 (summer 1966), pp. 151–74.

9. Friedan, *The Feminine Mystique*, p. 36.

10. See, for instance, the influential *The Mind Managers*, by Herbert I. Schiller, a collection of essays published in 1973. Schiller's book discusses "how the master puppeteers of politics, advertising, and mass communications pull the strings of public opinion." He does not, of course, specifically address gender differences among the "puppets." *The Mind Managers* (New York: Beacon Press, 1973).

11. A brief but useful overview of ideas about audience agency is provided by Sonia M. Livingston in "Audience Reception: The Role of the Viewer in Retelling Romantic Drama," in James Curran and Michael Gurevitch, eds., *Mass Media and Society* (New York: Edward Arnold, 1991), pp. 285–306. Although Livingstone studies the romance, and compares it generically with the soap opera, she does not raise the question of gender—either as a principle influencing interpretation or as one affecting the scholarly vision or expectations of audience roles and responses. For a discussion of the problem of feminist analysis of the media—which does not, however, apply these assumptions to any particular forms or contexts—see Liesbet van Zoonen, "Feminist Perspectives on the Media," in Curran and Gurevitch, *Mass Media and Society*, pp. 33–54.

12. Gaye Tuchman, "The Annihilation of Women by the Mass Media," in Gaye Tuchman, ed., *Hearth and Home: Images of Women in the Mass Media* (New York: Oxford University Press, 1977), pp. 3, 6.

13. Kathryn Weibel, *Mirror, Mirror: Images of Women Reflected in Popular Culture* (New York: Doubleday Anchor Press, 1977).

14. Marjorie Ferguson, *Forever Feminine: Women's Magazines and the Cult of Femininity* (London: Gower, 1983), p. 3.

15. Kathryn Shevelow, "Fathers and Daughters: Women As Readers of the Tatler," in Elizabeth Flynn and Patrocinio Schweickart, eds., *Gender and Reading: Essays on Readers, Texts and Contexts* (Baltimore: Johns Hopkins University Press, 1986), p. 108. See also Shevelow, *Women and Print Culture: The Construction of Femininity in the Early Periodical* (New York: Routledge, 1989).

16. Naomi Wolf, *The Beauty Myth: How Images of Beauty Are Used Against Women* (New York: William Morrow, 1991), p. 11.

17. "Landmark Study Reveals Women's Magazines Are Left-Wing Political Weapon," a report from The Media Research Center, Alexandria, VA, November 26, 1996.

18. Christina Hoff Sommers, "The Democrats' Secret Woman Weapon: In the Pages of Glossy Women's Magazines, the Party's Line Is in Fashion," *Washington Post*, National Weekly Edition, January 13, 1997, p. 22.

19. This most recent crop includes Danielle Crittenden, *What Our Mothers Didn't Tell Us: Why Happiness Eludes the Modern Woman* (New York: Simon & Schuster, 1999) and Wendy Shalit, *A Return to Modesty: Discovering the Lost Virtue* (New York: The Free Press, 1999). See also Alex Kuczynski, "Enough about Feminism. Should I Wear Lipstick?," *New York Times*, March 28, 1999, p. 4.

20. Crittenden, *What Our Mothers Didn't Tell Us*, p. 20–1.

21. Nathaniel Hawthorne's famous 1855 complaint to his publisher, George Ticknor, about the " d—d mob of scribbling women" is a key locus of this feeling on the part of men. For Hawthorne's comments on women writers, see Caroline Ticknor, *Hawthorne and His Publisher* (Boston: Houghton Mifflin Company, 1913). See also Ann Douglas, *The Feminization of American Culture* (New York: Alfred A. Knopf, 1977).

22. The first-generation feminist magazines consistently asserted this distinction. See, for example, "Not a Ladies' Magazine," in *Una*, Paulina Wright Davis, ed., February 1, 1853, p. 4.

23. Nina Baym, *Woman's Fiction: A Guide to Novels by and about Women, 1820–1870*. See also Helen Waite Papishvely, *All the Happy Endings* (New York: Harper and Co., 1956).

24. Ann (Wood) Douglas, "The 'Scribbling Women' and Fanny Fern: Why Women Wrote," *American Quarterly*, vol. 23, no. 1 (spring 1971), pp. 3–24.

25. John Tebbel and Mary Ellen Zuckerman, *The Magazine in America 1741–1990* (New York: Oxford University Press, 1991), p. 27.

26. Garnsey calculates this number at 110. See "Ladies Magazines to 1850." See also Stearns, "Before *Godey's*."

27. Okker has provided an invaluable index of these women and their editorial works. See the appendix to *Our Sister Editors: Sarah J. Hale and the Tradition of Nineteenth-Century American Women Editors* (Athens: University of Georgia Press, 1995).

28. The letter is cited by Lyon N. Richardson, *A History of Early American*

Magazines 1741–1789 (New York: Thomas Nelson and Sons, 1931), p. 1. Carl Bridenbaugh quotes what appears to be the same letter, which appeared with slightly changed wording in Webster's *American Magazine* (1787–88). See Bridenbaugh, "The Press and the Book in Eighteenth Century Philadelphia," *Pennsylvania Magazine of History and Biography*, vol. 65, no. 1 (January 1941), pp. 1–31.

29. See Dorothy Foster, "The Earliest Precursor of Our Present-Day Monthly Miscellanies," *PMLA*, vol. 32, no. 1 (1917), pp. 22–58.

30. Mott says that "the Addisonian essay was a chief stock in trade of the eighteenth century magazine" and also comments that "the four most important magazines [from the Revolution to the end of the eighteenth century] . . . , the *Columbian Magazine* and the *American Museum*, of Philadelphia, the *Massachusetts Magazine*, of Boston, and the *New-York Magazine*," are notable for their "eclecticism." See Mott, *A History of American Magazines, Vol. 1: 1741–1850*, pp. 41, 30, 39.

31. M.M. Bakhtin, *The Dialogic Imagination* (Austin: University of Texas Press, 1981).

32. Horace Newcombe, "On the Dialogic Aspects of Mass Communication," in Robert K. Avery and David Eason, eds., *Critical Perspectives on Media and Society* (London: Guilford Press, 1992).

33. Mott describes the eighteenth century as the "lean years" in magazine production, and cites the indifference of readers and writers, lack of adequate means of distribution, losses in the collection of subscription fees, and manufacturing embarrassments in explaining the cessation rate of periodicals. Mott, *A History of American Magazines, Vol. 1: 1741–1850*, p. 13. See also Richardson, *The American Magazine 1741–1789*.

34. See Kenneth Cmeil, *Democratic Eloquence: The Fight Over Popular Speech in Nineteenth Century America* (New York: William Morrow, 1990). Regarding the diversifying marketplace, see Richard D. Brown, "From Cohesion to Competition," and Rhys Isaac, "Books and the Authority of Learning: The Case of Mid-Eighteenth-Century Virginia," both in Joyce, Hall, Brown and Heinrich, eds., *Printing and Society in Early America* (Worcester, MA: American Antiquarian Society, 1983).

35. These examples are drawn from the August 1996 issue of *Glamour*, which is published by the Conde Nast Corporation. The fertility treatment versus Planned Parenthood juxtaposition appears on p. 108; the diet pills piece versus the supermodel ad on p. 42.

36. An excellent discussion of race and illiteracy is Dana Nelson Solvino, "The Word in Black and White: Ideologies of Race and Literacy in Antebellum America," in Cathy Davidson, ed., *Reading in America: Literature and Social History* (Baltimore: Johns Hopkins University Press, 1989), pp. 140–56.

37. Five solid introductions to the African American presses are Frankie Hutton, *The Early Black Press in America, 1827–1860* (Westport, CT: Greenwood Press, 1993); I. Garland Penn, *The Afro-American Press and Its Editors* (New York:

Arno Press and *New York Times*, 1969); Roland E. Wolseley, *The Black Press, U.S.A.* (Ames: Iowa State University Press, 1971); Penelope Bullock, *The Afro-American Press, 1838–1909* (New York: Oxford University Press, 1978); Walter C. Daniels, *Black Journals of the U.S.* (Westport, CT: Greenwood Press, 1982); and Armistead Scott Pride, "A Register and History of Negro Newspapers in the U.S., 1827–1950" (Ph.D. diss., Northwestern University, 1950).

38. Lori Ginzberg discusses this relationship in *Women and the Work of Benevolence: Morality, Politics and Class in the Nineteenth-Century United States* (New Haven: Yale University Press, 1990).

39. Mott writes that most American magazine subscriptions sold for $2.50 per year in 1790. The cost of Franklin's *General Magazine* "was the equivalent of from one to one-and-one-half sacks of flour in the Philadelphia market. Or it would buy from one and a half to two bushels of wheat." In terms of wages, he continues, "a carpenter would have to spend the wages of three or four days" for a magazine subscription and "a farm laborer would have to work four or five days to earn enough to pay a year's subscription." See Mott, A *History of American Magazines, Vol. 1 : 1741–1850*, pp. 33–4.

40. Cathy Davidson notes that a carpenter in Massachusetts earned $1.00 per day in 1800, and an unskilled laborer about half that much. For this price, one could buy a bushel of potatoes, half a bushel of corn, about a yard-and-a-half of cotton cloth, or two pairs of leather shoes. See Davidson, *Revolution and the Word: The Rise of the Novel in America* (New York: Oxford University Press, 1986), pp. 24–5.

41. Michael Warner cite from Chapter 3.

42. See Carl F. Kaestle, "The History of Literacy and the History of Readers," *Review of Research in Education*, vol. 12 (1985), pp. 11–53. See also William J. Gilmore, *Elementary Literacy on the Eve of the Industrial Revolution: Trends in Rural New England, 1760–1830* (Worcester, MA: American Antiquarian Society, 1982).

43. See Ellen McCracken, *Decoding Women's Magazines: From Mademoiselle to Ms.* (New York: St. Martin's Press, 1993), particularly "Reaching Minority Women: Language, Culture and Politics in the Service of Consumerism," pp. 223–56, in which she discusses the uses of hegemonic policing in *Essence, Latina*, and other "ethnic" women's magazines.

44. Cathy Davidson, "Towards a History of Books and Readers," *American Quarterly*, vol. 40, no. 2 (June 1988), p. 11. See also David Paul Nord, "A Republican Literature: A Study of Magazine Reading and Readers in Late Eighteenth-Century New York," *American Quarterly*, vol. 40, no. 2 (June 1988), pp. 85–101.

45. The issue of diversity in the women's movement is the explicit concern of a growing field of writing by a new generation of feminist women. See, for example, Rebecca Walker, ed., *To Be Real: Telling the Truth and Changing the Face of Feminism* (New York: Anchor Books, 1995) and Barbara Findlen, ed., *Listen Up: Voices from the Next Feminist Generation* (Seattle: Seal Press, 1995/2002).

46. See William Henry Chafe, *The American Woman: Her Changing Social, Economic and Political Roles, 1920–1970* (New York: Oxford University Press, 1972).

47. See Nancy A. Walker's introduction to her anthology, *Women's Magazines 1940–1960: Gender Roles and the Popular Press* (New York: St. Martin's, 1998) and her *Shaping Our Mothers' World: American Women's Magazines* (Jackson: University of Mississippi Press, 2000). Other more nuanced treatments of content and its reception include Jennifer Scanlon, *Inarticulate Longings: The Ladies' Home Journal, Gender, and the Promises of Consumer Culture* (New York: Routledge, 1995) and Helen Damon-Moore, *Magazines for the Millions: Gender and Commerce in the Ladies' Home Journal and the Saturday Evening Post, 1880–1910* (Albany: SUNY Press, 1994). Even Friedan herself notes that she leaves several columns out of her analysis, including regular columns by Eleanor Roosevelt and Clare Booth Luce, as well as "Pats and Pans," the reader letters column. See *The Feminine Mystique*, pp. 35–6.

48. This bias, of course, may result from the fact that so much of this research is being pursued in English departments, where "high" literary texts are more often the subject of interest. Still, see, for example, Judith Fetterly, *The Resisting Reader: A Feminist Approach to American Fiction* (Bloomington: Indiana University Press, 1978). See also Elizabeth Flynn and Patrocinio Schweickart, whose excellent anthology, *Gender and Reading: Essays on Readers, Texts and Contexts* (Baltimore: Johns Hopkins University Press, 1986) nevertheless does at times reflect this slant.

49. See, for example, Thomas Leonard, *News for All: America's Coming-of-Age with the Press* (New York: Oxford University Press, 1995).

50. See, for example, editor Carl F. Kaestle's essay, "The History of Readers," in Carl F. Kaestle, Helen Damon-Moore, Lawrence C. Stedman, Katherine Tinsley, and William Vance Trollinger Jr., eds., *Literacy in the United States: Readers and Reading Since 1880* (New Haven: Yale University Press, 1991).

51. Helen Damon-Moore and Carl F. Kaestle, "Gender, Advertising and Mass-Circulation Magazines," in Carl Kaestle et al., eds., *Literacy in the United States*, pp. 245–71.

52. As Joke Hermes discusses, "The small but steady stream of publications about women's magazines has, until recently, hardly ever taken the perspective of the experiences of the reader into account." Hermes offers a useful summary of this research, which by his account spans the years from 1978 to 1991. See Hermes, *Reading Women's Magazines* (Cambridge, UK: Polity Press, 1995), particularly pp. 10–7. See also Liesbet Van Zoonen, "Feminist Perspectives on the Mass Media," in Curran and Gurevitch, eds., *Mass Media and Society* (London: Edward Arnold, 1992).

53. Stuart Hall, "Encoding/Decoding," in Stuart Hall et al., eds., *Culture, Media, Language* (London: Hutchinson, 1980), p. 134.

54. Ellen Garvey, *The Adman in the Parlor: Mass-Market Women's Magazines*

and the Gendering of Consumer Culture (New York: Oxford University Press, 1996).

55. "Disturber of the Peace: Ayn Rand"; Virginia Moss, "15 Girls Who Correct Harvard Men"; "Clothes Men Love"; Robert Laxalt, "We Could Make Such Beautiful Mayonnaise Together," *Mademoiselle*, May 1962, pp. 172, 176, 126, 78.

56. Phyllis McGinley, "Ten Ways to Keep a Husband—Young Profession: Housewife," *Ladies' Home Journal*, January 1963, p. 87.

57. Dr. Spock, "Should Mothers Work?," *Ladies' Home Journal*, January 1963, pp. 16, 18, 21.

58. Betty Friedan, "Angry Letters: Readers Reply to the Charge of 'The Fraud of Femininity,'" *McCall's*, August 1962, pp. 38, 40, 165.

59. "Our Readers Write Us," *Ladies' Home Journal*, April 1963, p. 20. It's important to note the editorial framing of the letters, however. "As this issue goes to press, four out of five of hundreds of readers who've written us say that Betty Friedan is wrong."

60. Stanley Fish, *Is There a Text in This Class? The Authority of Interpretive Communities* (Cambridge: Harvard University Press, 1980). See also Elizabeth Long, "Women, Reading and Cultural Authority: Some Implications of the Audience Perspective in Cultural Studies," *American Quarterly* 38 (fall 1986), pp. 606–10. Finally, Cathy Davidson's brief overview of "The Sociology of Reading Communities" is also helpful. See Davidson, ed., *Reading in America: Literature and Social History*, pp. 18–22.

61. Michael Schudson, "The New Validation of Popular Culture: Sense and Sentimentality in Academia," in Robert K. Avery and David Eason, eds., *Critical Perspectives on Media and Society* (London: Guilford Press, 1992), pp. 48–68.

62. Alexis de Tocqueville, *Democracy in America* (New York: Harper & Row, 1966), pp. 517–20.

63. John Fiske, "Postmodernism and Television," in James Curran and Michael Gurevitch, eds., *Mass Media and Society* (New York: Edward Arnold, 1992).

CHAPTER 1

Taking Liberties: "Democracy" and Dynamics in America's Magazines

The frontispiece to William Gibbons's *Ladies Magazine and Repository of Entertaining and Instructive Knowledge* (1792–93), the first American women's magazine, offers a provocative vision of the goal—or at least the selling point—of the form at its origin. We are told in a caption that the engraving depicts the "Genius of the Ladies Magazine." It portrays two female figures, both draped in the Grecian garb reflective of the classical and mythic proportions in which the new nation was often envisioned in the eighteenth century. One of the female figures is seated slightly above the other. This higher figure displays post-Revolutionary and "masculine" markers of patriotism: she holds a flag, and at her side rests a shield. This figure is labeled "Liberty." The second figure carries a laurel crown and kneels at the feet of Liberty, looking upward into her face, like a child smiling expectantly into its mother's eyes. She is the "Genius of Emulation." The two women are shown to be in a process of exchange. One hands the other an unfurling scroll, which occupies the absolute center of the drawing. As both Liberty and Emulation stretch out their hands to grasp it, the unfolding text reveals its title: *The Rights of Woman*.

This cover art for the first American women's magazine mixes national identity with gender iconography, waving the genre as both the sign and the site of unfurling women's rights in the American public.[1] Its integration of "masculine" liberties and rights with "feminine" nurturance and emulation, all surrounding a central image of collaboration and exchange, suggests that the magazine itself will carry the democratic process to women. Working textually (as a forum for competing discourses), socially (as a meeting ground for multiple contributors), and symbolically (as the site where Liberty is expressed, emulated, and reproduced through maternal nurture), women's magazines were to be places for participation that echoed—and in some ways overlapped—popular ideas of democracy at the time. They set themselves up as the means to self-representation and collective participation denied by the customs of the country's founding fathers.

Women's magazines could sell themselves as "democracy" not only because that was one thing prospective readers may have wanted to hear, but because magazines in general had significant stature within the early American press. And by the middle decades of the eighteenth century, the press had become "integrated . . . with an emergent republican paradigm as the proper medium of the public."[2] Indeed, in the secular Eastern cities where the first women's magazines appeared, prevailing understandings characterized print publication and the press "as indispensable to political life . . . [and] the primary agent of world emancipation."[3]

The earliest women's magazines were therefore part authentic cultural politics, part democratic hoopla—and part canny commercial insight about how these factors could influence emerging markets. Although they were not explicitly commercial—little advertising typically appeared beyond the occasional notices of books for sale in printers' bookshops—women's magazines helped propel the emerging free enterprise culture of letters, in which self-made print tradesmen and democratizing press law together were expanding and recharacterizing the way print was conceived and consumed. Trends in women's increasing literacy and (for some) leisure both fed and followed from these shifts, particularly in the cosmopolitan centers. Thus, American women's magazines, a signal product of the developing "democratic free market society,"[4] became pioneers in making the political popular—and vice versa. This gave women an in.

LITERARY ECONOMICS MEETS CULTURAL POLITICS: THE ALL-AMERICAN MAGAZINE

In America, the magazine was both a product and a vehicle of emergent democracy. Born in 1741, the form arose amidst a changing relationship of people to print. The "democratization of print" described by Elizabeth Eisenstein and others basically entails the unseating of the privileged classes as the exclusive keepers of knowledge.[5]

The American magazine was also born of marketplace competition. Its first producers, Philadelphia's Benjamin Franklin and Andrew Bradford, had been rivals since their early days in newspaper publishing in the 1730s. The two announced plans for their respective magazines at virtually the same instant, and they rushed their designs into production—with

Bradford stealing Franklin's intended editor, one John Webbe, along the way—to arrive on the literary marketplace only three days apart. Although the two periodicals each carried the publication date January 1741, Bradford's *American Magazine, or A Monthly View of the Political State of the British Colonies*, appeared first, on February 13, 1741, beating Franklin's *General Magazine, and Historical Chronicle, For all the British Plantations in America* to the punch.[6]

Franklin's *General Magazine* was the better value to readers, though, as it ran to 75 pages in six-point type—more than twice the length of Bradford's 32-page, ten-point-sized production—for about the same price: the *General Magazine* sold for ninepence, whereas Bradford charged eightpence sterling (one shilling, Pennsylvania currency). Both magazines were a bargain, especially in light of where prices soon went. By the Revolutionary era, American magazines cost between $2.25 per year, the price of Thomas and James Swords's well-read *New-York Magazine* (1790–97), and $3.33 per year, the price of Mathew Carey's lengthier *American Museum* (1787–92).[7]

Like most colonial magazines to come, both the *American Magazine* and the *General Magazine* covered mainly official information—schedules, announcements, and pronouncements of various kinds—although Franklin offered more content variety,[8] and also carried more advertising.[9] And, both expired quickly. Bradford published three issues of his monthly; Franklin only six. Indeed, Franklin's venture was so short-lived and unprofitable that he omitted it entirely from his *Autobiography of Benjamin Franklin*.

The rapid failure of the first American magazines is not surprising. As Frank Luther Mott has described, magazine publishing in colonial and early America was only a break-even proposition in the best case. On average, circulations ran only in the hundreds before about 1820.[10] Indeed, the innovator and educator Noah Webster, who edited the ambitious *American Magazine* (1787–88), remarked that "the expectation of failure is connected with the very name of the magazine."[11] Yet, whatever their commercial disappointments at first, the overall fortunes of the magazine's first publishers remain rich in implications.

Bradford and Franklin can be seen as contrasting eighteenth-century types, representing two competing claims to the profession of print. Andrew Bradford was born with a printing pedigree that extended back at least three generations, as well as across the Atlantic to the capital cities of Europe. Paternal grandson of a successful London printer, maternal grandson of another London printer, and son of William Bradford, official printer of Pennsylvania from 1685 to 1693, Andrew was born into one of the prominent print dynasties that dominated the trade from the colonies to the Revolutionary era.[12]

The dynastic structure of the trade was inherited from European practice, and maintained by law, customs, and the costs of doing business. Barriers to newcomers included government licensure, extensive training, and social practices, such as apprenticeship agreements and marriages among print families. Andrew Bradford himself married into the London-based Sowle family to which he had been apprenticed, thereby strengthening the kinship system that underpinned the business. Moreover, significant start-up capital was required to purchase a printing press and complete set of types, and necessary materials, such as paper and ink, were manufactured commodities, which then as now were far more expensive to obtain than the raw materials needed in other skilled trades.[13]

As a result, even though the overall practice of print expanded dramatically in the colonies during the era that gave rise to the magazine, entrepreneurial opportunity did not. Between 1720 and 1760, the number of newspapers published rose from just three to more than twenty. The number of master printers also grew: in Philadelphia, from only one in 1720 to nine in 1760; in New York, from one to five during that time; in Boston, from six to fourteen. Elsewhere in the colonies, just one print shop was joined by thirteen others during that time.[14] Still, fewer than one in three printers' apprentices went on to own and run print shops competitive with the established houses during those years.[15] The printing trade after 1720 may have grown "much faster than even the population,"[16] until the Revolutionary era, yet it remained an insider business bound by blood.

Benjamin Franklin was the exception to the old rules. As a newcomer in Philadelphia, he had neither a prestigious family history nor family money with which to enter the printing trade. Indeed, whereas Bradford entered the business seemingly by birthright, Franklin became a printer largely by default: he tried his hand at printing to appease his father, who begged him not to seek his fortunes at sea.[17] Later, Franklin unexpectedly became a newspaper editor when his older brother, James, jailed for publishing material offensive to the Boston clerical establishment in his *New-England Courant* (1721–27), suddenly left young Benjamin, then fifteen, as temporary proprietor of the paper.

The teenage Franklin had had less than a year's experience with *The Courant* when he took the helm. He had had only brief apprenticeship experience in newspapering before that, as the Franklin shop had printed the *Boston Gazette* for a short time in 1719–20. And he was fully self-taught as a "compositor," or printer-writer; he describes in his auto-biography that he trained himself in writing and rhetoric by his repeated readings of the popular British magazine the *Spectator*.[18] Whereas Bradford's career as a printer capitalized on two generations of family expertise, prestige, and capital, Franklin began broke, with little more than a boyhood enjoyment of a popular British miscellany and a brief apprenticeship with his brother's dangerously Republican newspaper.

But Franklin did have moxie and an unusual business sense, as his early experiences in Philadelphia printing reveal. He quickly appreciated the business weaknesses of his first employer, Samuel Keimer, noting that his boss "kept his shop miserably, sold often without Profit for ready Money, . . . often trusted without keeping Accounts," and "was in debt for all he possess'd."[19] Since Franklin also observed that this poor management kept Keimer's creditors "uneasy," he purchased his own press and types from London, quit Keimer, and opened a rival print shop in Philadelphia as soon as he was able. He formed a partnership with Hugh Meredith, another Keimer employee, proposing to furnish his valuable "Skill in the Business" while Meredith was to put up the start-up capital. The profits would be shared equally in the new venture.[20]

The Franklin shop saw relatively rapid success, and as soon as it did, the ambitious young printer set his sights on a riskier venture—but one promising big returns and even bigger community stature: a newspaper. Having written for Andrew Bradford's *American Weekly Mercury* (1719–46) in the 1720s, Franklin was in a position to observe that the paper was "a paltry thing, wretchedly manag'd, and no way entertaining; and yet was profitable to him."[21] Franklin's rival newspaper, the *Pennsylvania Gazette* (1727–49), drew on unprecedented amounts of advertising revenue and the literary skill of its editor to rapidly become the cornerstone of the only print shop in Philadelphia capable of competing with Bradford's.[22]

It did not take long for Franklin's former employers to castigate him as a thief and a dishonorable man, but his business ethics, for better or worse, were perfectly in tune with the changing times. Franklin's success speaks to the shift from European, aristocratic traditions—represented by the privileged and pedigreed Bradford—to the colonies' more individualistic, mercantile mind-set preeminently demonstrated by Franklin.[23] The American magazine, born of this transition, reflects in its very structure and concept this changing climate of American print: its variety and polyvocality bespeak the shift from regulated production in which participation and profits were controlled by an inbred elite, to a more open competition marked by decentralization, flexibility, and individual hustle.

Bradford the aristocrat; Franklin the democrat. In the divergent business strategies stemming from this discrepant status, the two printers figured the future of the trade. Bradford developed his business through his family's extended network of familial contacts in the colonies, in England, and elsewhere; Franklin continued to grow his business through joint ventures and silent partnerships with associates along the eastern seaboard.[24] By the Revolutionary era, the kind of joint-venture partnerships pioneered by Franklin had become the standard in practice for the most successful American printers.[25] Franklin also created intrabusiness partnerships with related industries such as papermaking and typecasting, as if foreseeing corporate enterprise far in America's future.[26]

Yet the massive institutional restructuring that conditioned the qualities of the American magazine could never have resulted merely from individual talent and enterprise—no matter what time-honored American mythologies about self-made men might suggest. Political and legal strictures were changing at the same time. English law that had regulated the British print trade since the sixteenth century had governed colonial printing as well—until the era in which the American magazine emerged.

Strict licensing laws instituted by Henry Tudor in 1529 remained the most direct form of press control in the American colonies into the eighteenth century. Colonial printers published "By Authority"—that is, by license from governing powers. Although these licensure laws had expired in England in 1695 with Parliament's refusal to renew the Printing Act, colonial governors "continued to receive standardized instructions from London . . . advising that prior approval of all publications be required" until at least 1730.[27] It was by prosecution of this power that James Franklin was imprisoned in 1723 and forced to turn over his *New-England Courant* to his brother Benjamin, pressing the younger Franklin into his career as a printer, editor, writer, and more.

As the restrictive potential of licensing regulations diminished, other governmental instruments of press control were adopted more locally. Printers could be called before colonial legislative agencies, which held broad judicial powers to level less-than-specific charges, including "affronts," "impudence," "indignities," and "breach of privilege," or "contempt."[28] The kingpin of this family of charges was "seditious libel," which, although it was hardly distinguishable from other discretionary charges,[29] was particularly deployed against those who printed material critical of governing powers. Such charges often resulted in serious punishment, even imprisonment. Four cases of seditious libel were prosecuted in the colonies prior to the precedent-setting 1735 acquittal of John Peter

Zenger, printer of the New York *Weekly Journal*, which effectively established for the public—if not for another fifty years in the law books—that the truth of a published statement was an adequate defense against a claim of libel.

Seditious libel prosecutions continued through 1798, although they were rare.[30] But for both Franklin and Bradford, familial experiences almost surely kept the threat alive and close to mind. The very first case of seditious libel ever brought in the colonies was against then Philadelphia printer William Bradford, Andrew's father. Bradford the elder was brought to trial in December of 1692 by the Quakers of Philadelphia, for whom he had emigrated to the colonies to work, for publishing a pamphlet, "An Appeal from the Twenty-Eight Judges to the Spirit of Truth." This confrontation with the Quaker authorities was not the first of Bradford's difficulties arising from the products of his presses; at least five of his earliest publications met with objections from the Society of Friends.[31] Released on account of what would now be called a hung jury,[32] the elder Bradford departed in the spring of 1693 to try his fortunes in New York. Once he arrived, however, he antagonized yet another colonial governor, the Earl of Bellomont, who briefly debarred the senior Bradford from receiving his salary as public printer.

The younger Bradford followed in his father's footsteps in this kind of print activity, too. Andrew suffered government reprimand by the authorities of Pennsylvania in 1722 (just prior to James Franklin's imprisonment for "Breach of Authority"), and in 1729, Andrew, like his father before him, went to prison for printing matter obnoxious to the government.[33] Andrew Bradford lost his government printing work to Ben Franklin, his enterprising young rival now in his own business.

Even as these laws relaxed during the eighteenth century, governmental authorities wielded economic pressure that continued to control, or at least curtail, the printing business. The Crown taxed printed materials for a time (only to explode in the Stamp Act protests of 1765–66), and subsidies for official printing contracts were common by about midcentury.[34] Even though government job printing was not sufficient to sustain a printer's business by this time, official contracts were valuable for their relative regularity and for their reliability over an extended term. Plus, government contracts carried sufficient cachet (less problematically before the Revolutionary era) to sometimes generate new business from organizations, quasi-official groups, and prominent individuals.[35]

Yet garnering government work also exacted a price. To win a government contract, printers were expected to toe the party line, refusing business from groups or individuals critical of or running contrary to officialdom. As the regulatory conditions surrounding the printing trade began to change, and both institutional and occupational structures shifted accordingly, colonial printers found themselves facing contradictory demands. On the one hand, an amiable relationship with governing powers, both at home and in England, remained a source of dependable income and professional stature. But authorities in the colonies were constantly shifting and unstable, which undercut these potential benefits considerably. Plus, private customers, whose diverse voices couldn't help but run aground of some colonial authority or other, were beginning to look like the growth sector of the business. As trade expansion put print shops into increasing competition with one another, garnering these individual customers became crucial to success. What print tradesman could afford to resist the wave of the future, especially for only uncertain commitments and a partial living offered by official work in the clearly changing present?

MAGAZINE DEMOCRACY IN THE MAKING:
THE POLITICS AND PROFITS OF PRESS LIBERTY

It was in response to this shifting political economy in the trade that colonial printers began to call for "press liberty." As Stephen Botein has described, the "first priority [of government printers in the colonies] was to serve the authorities satisfactorily," but "there were good business reasons to want to serve other political groups, even those critical of the government."[36] Although put forth in political terms, the first notions of the "free press" were inspired as much by the profit motive as by the genius of democracy. As Botein continues, "Embedded in the prevailing colonial rhetoric concerning 'liberty of the press' was a principle readily embraced by much of the trade—that printers should be politically neutral in the conduct of their businesses, and publish whatever was submitted to them."[37]

"Press liberty" was perhaps the one occupational idea on which Franklin and Bradford agreed. Both had learned in their tender years of their vulnerability to harassment and of the need for savvy if they hoped to publish and survive, let alone profit.[38] It was Bradford's own newspaper, the *American Weekly Mercury*, that carried Franklin's 1729 essay in which the author, though veiled by his "Busy-Body" persona, asserted that printers do not speak for "any Party more than any other" in their work.[39]

Franklin's "Apology for Printers," published first in the June 10, 1731, issue of his own *Pennsylvania Gazette*, went much further, offering a sustained argument for this idea of printers' relationship to copy and customers. The "Apology" begins on democratic grounds, but soon turns to include a business rationale. Franklin first argues that public debate is both right and advantageous, and that the open press of printers should enable that process: "Printers are educated in the Belief that when Men differ in Opinion, both Sides ought equally to have the Advantage of being heard by the Publick." He continues, evoking the climate of competition and free enterprise: "In the way of their Business, they print such great variety of things opposite and contradictory." Diversity of views, rather than authoritative control—by anyone—makes the most sense, in his view: "it is . . . unreasonable what some assert, *That Printers ought not print any Thing but what they approve;* since . . . an End would thereby be put to Free Writing, and the World afterwards have nothing to read but what happen'd to be the Opinions of Printers."

The "Apology" started a wave of newspaper and magazine contributions through the 1740s—the very decade in which the first American magazines appeared. These many articles instigated and spread ideas about what press liberty should be, and why it should prevail in the colonies. What's more, the ostensibly participatory process by which these ideas were developed and validated in colonial newspapers demonstrates the mechanisms of popularization and legitimization that were inherited and put to use by women in their magazines.

It was in 1741, the year of the magazine's birth, that printer Thomas Fleet wrote an "Apology" of his own in the *Boston Post-Boy.* Having printed John Wesley's controversial "Sermon on Free Grace," Fleet explains in terms consistent with Franklin's that "For my own part, as I have declar'd, so I do again declare, that I am of no Party, but act purely as a *Printer,* and would as soon serve one Side as the other." Echoing Franklin's words as well as his shift from political to economic claims, Fleet continues, "I printed Mr. Wesley's Sermon not because I liked it, but because several Gentlemen of Good Sense and Learning . . . desired to have it printed, and I had a prospect of getting a Penny by it, as I have by all that I print, having no other Way to support my Family, and to pay what the Church and State expect from me."[40] Fleet, writing later than Franklin, strategically addresses the specific economic interests of the organizing state itself. If his presses were restricted, he asserts, he could neither feed his family nor pay his taxes to the local government.

Thereafter, numerous versions and revisions of the notion of press liberty appeared in periodicals throughout the colonies. Some were explicitly written by printers; others appeared anonymously—although these, too, could have been written by printers or their colleagues. Jeremiah Gridley, attorney general of Massachusetts and former editor of Boston's *Weekly*

Rehearsal (1731–32), submitted a lengthy essay on the subject of press freedom that appeared in the inaugural issue of the Boston-based *American
Magazine and Historical Chronicle* (1743–46); an anonymous contribution
to the premiere issue of Boston's *Independent Advertiser* further refined the
concept in 1744. The theme spread, inciting two anonymous submissions
on the subject in the *New-York Mercury* of October and December of
1754, both of which inspired continued attention, either through subsequent responses or by pirated reprints.[41] (Reprints appeared in Franklin's
Pennsylvania Gazette of December 12, 1754, and in the *Virginia Gazette*
of March 7, 1755.) Franklin kept the process going by republishing his
original "Apology" in a variety of popular formats, including a versified
version in his enormously popular *Poor Richard's Almanac* in 1749. This
and other versions circulated widely, and were pirated or excerpted elsewhere in the colonies, such as in the major papers of both Maryland and
South Carolina (where the editors were business associates of Franklin's)
thereafter.[42]

Since the concept of a free press was developed and circulated through
the public participation of many voices, it seemed to emerge from the very
democratic culture it promised to vouchsafe. The successful evolution and
authorization of press liberty is the first, best example of the constructive
capabilities and legitimizing power of the popular press in early America—
capabilities that the first women's magazines used to similarly develop and
ratify new discourse for public use.

Although there appeared to be widespread agreement about the need
for press liberty, there was less consensus about how this liberty should
be enacted on the printed page. Just as audiences take away different possibilities from their reading of texts, different colonial printers understood
and employed press freedom in different ways. Franklin, for his part, opted
for a debate model, or juridical model, which implied the publication of
opinion on both sides of an issue.[43] To accomplish such balance, he either
solicited or would write the contrapuntal view, presenting any self-
authored entries either anonymously or under a pseudonym. This "open
forum" approach, as it was called, first appeared in weekly and monthly
Advertisers in the 1730s.[44] This approach corroborates the idea of "dis-
interested exchange" theorized by Jürgen Habermas as the leading quality of the public.[45] In a more applied sense, it also may be the earliest
precursor of the concept of "objectivity" in modern journalism.[46]

Other printers saw press liberty—and audiences—differently. Thomas
Fleet's vision of a free press more closely resembled today's "tabloid" style,
complete with its idea of a controversy-hungry public, eager for un-

censored access to the inside or underside of issues. Fleet deliberately selected controversial matters to publish, contriving thereby to provoke scandal, gossip, even outrage—anything that might promote purchases. For him, press freedom meant publishing anything that he bet the public would pay to read; printer "neutrality" meant he need not act as a moral guardian or intellectual guide of the public interest or taste. The intentional publication of provocative material had proved a lucrative strategy for many of Britain's Grub Street authors and publishers by the 1730s, and Fleet maintained enough transatlantic business ties to have sensed the value of this approach on the American scene.[47]

Still other colonial printers chose risk aversion as the route to relief from repressive intervention and to public approval. As Botein explains, some printers in the 1740s and '50s "excluded the more censorious effusions of all parties." "The result," Botein describes, "was not receptivity but even-handed aversion to diverse and forceful opinions."[48]

This was Andrew Bradford's approach. His prospectus for the *American Magazine*, published in the October 30–November 6, 1740, issue of his *Weekly Mercury* newspaper, emphasizes that the printer's very absence would be his magazine's definitive strategy and major selling point. "We shall *inviolably* observe the exact Neutrality," Bradford assures his readers, "and *carefully* avoid mingling with the Arguments on either Side, and Reflections or Remarks of our own."[49]

Paradoxically, this approach at once de-politicizes and potentially democratizes the American magazine. The printer's absence from organizing content, and from editorializing within the publication, renders the magazine an open book, in which a variety of contributor voices and viewpoints could be written and read. "The Reader is desired to consider the Undertaking, as an Attempt to *Erect*, on *Neutral Principles*, a PUBLIC THEATRE in the *Center of the British Empire in America*," Bradford concludes.

Bradford's idea of the magazine makes it close kin to the undifferentiated, participatory eighteenth-century American theater.[50] The form is conceived as an interactive stage on which—like Franklin's famous stagecoach metaphor for democracy from the *Autobiography*[51]—any and every citizen can be a player. Although seemingly nonpartisan and apolitical, Bradford constructs a kind of democratic forum; his magazine trusts in the ongoing cycle of audience participation, of contribution and feedback over time, to determine an agenda as well as standards of speech and conduct. He makes the American magazine a site of community progress through citizen rule.

In the context of these three predominant approaches, early American women's magazines can be seen as about as good an expression of the American free press as one can get. Most magazines were so "democratic" that all three approaches were at play within them at the same time. They entertained the cross-examination of conventional expectations and practices (as Franklin might have expected); exposed as scandalous various common practices (as Fleet might have preferred); and were an audience-driven meeting ground for the exchange of advice, support, and fellow-feeling (as Bradford envisioned).

The juxtaposition of these approaches may have been intended to depoliticize, to trivialize the genre in an Early Republic where a "masculine," strictly partisan political press reigned.[52] However, what it actually created was a *very* free press environment, in which range of discourse could play freely and constructively over time. For women, this kind of space helped entertain many modes of women's self-representation—from self-expression to debate, from questioning, to social critique, to consensus-building. And all the while, it helped legitimate both efforts and outcomes due to their origins in a popular venue seen as both testament and instrument of democracy in America.

NOTES

1. Frank Luther Mott describes that national pride was tied up with the motivation for producing early magazines and was often used to apply to the public for support. See Mott, *A History of American Magazines, Vol. 1: 1741–1850* (New York: D. Appleton and Company, 1930), p. 23.

2. This is Michael Warner's thesis in *Letters of the Republic: Publication and the Public Sphere in Eighteenth Century America* (Cambridge: Harvard University Press, 1990), p. 33.

3. Ibid.

4. Michael Schudson, *Discovering the News: A Social History of American Newspapers* (New York: Basic Books, 1978), pp. 12–60.

5. See Elizabeth Eisenstein, *The Printing Press As an Agent of Change* (Cambridge: Cambridge University Press, 1980).

6. Mott provides brief sketches of the two magazines in *A History of American Magazines, Vol. 1: 1741–1850*, pp. 73–7 (*General Magazine*); pp. 80–2 (*American Magazine*).

7. Ibid., pp. 33–4.

8. Ibid., pp. 71–7.

9. Franklin had been running a significant amount of advertising in his *Pennsylvania Gazette* for more than a decade when he produced the first ad ever to run in an American magazine—a notice about the Philadelphia ferry schedule—

for the May 10 issue of his *General Magazine*. See Mott, *A History of American Magazines*, *Vol. 1*, pp. 34–5.

10. Mott notes that fewer than 100 magazines were attempted before 1825 and that there were "no successful national publications" before that era. See Mott, *A History of American Magazines*, *Vol: 1*, pp. 341–2, 200.

11. The comment is quoted in Mott, *A History of American Magazines*, *Vol. 1*, p. 11. See also Mott's sketch of the *American Magazine* in the same volume of the history, pp. 104–7.

12. The Bradfords were as powerful in the colonial printing trade in the middle colonies as the Green family was in the New England region. Douglas C. McMurtie maps the landscape of colonial print dynasties in *A History of Printing in the United States*, *Vol. 2: Middle and South Atlantic States* (New York: R.R. Bowker Co., 1936).

13. Peter J. Parker, "The Philadelphia Printer: A Study of an Eighteenth-Century Businessman," *Business History Review*, vol. 40, no. 1 (1966), p. 24.

14. Stephen Botein, "'Meer Mechanics' and an Open Press: The Business and Political Strategies of Colonial American Printers," *Perspectives in American History*, vol. 9 (1975). See also Warner, *Letters of the Republic*, p. 32.

15. Botein, "'Meer Mechanics' and an Open Press," pp. 150, 134.

16. Warner, *Letters of the Republic*, pp. 32–3.

17. Albert Furtwangler, "Franklin's Apprenticeship and the *Spectator*," *New England Quarterly*, vol. 52, no. 3 (September 1979), p. 378.

18. Through persistent imitation of editors Steele and Addison, and redactions of content in various formats, Franklin learned that he might "possibly in time become a tolerable English writer." Benjamin Franklin, *The Autobiography of Benjamin Franklin* (New Haven: Yale University Press, 1964), p. 62.

19. Franklin, *Autobiography*, p. 66.

20. Ibid., p. 67.

21. Ibid., p. 75.

22. In addition to Franklin's account of the events in his *Autobiography*, see McMurtie, *A History of Printing in the United States*, pp. 1–54.

23. As Michael Warner notes, Franklin's "career corresponds in striking detail to the path of the press's expansion." See Warner, *Letters of the Republic*, p. 75.

24. See McMurtie, *A History of Printing in the United States*, p. 39. See also Richard D. Brown, "Afterword: From Cohesion to Competition," in Joyce, Hall, Brown, and Heinrich, eds., *Printing and Society in Early America* (Worcester, MA: American Antiquarian Society, 1983), p. 305.

25. Parker, "The Philadelphia Printer," p. 42.

26. Warner, *Letters of the Republic*, p. 76

27. Botein, "'Meer Mechanics' and an Open Press," p. 127

28. Harold L. Nelson, "Seditious Libel in Colonial America," *The American Journal of Legal History*, vol. 3 (1959), p. 163.

29. Ibid., p. 165.

30. Michael Emery and Edwin Emery, *The Press and America: An Interpretive History of the Mass Media* (Boston: Allyn & Bacon, 1996), p. 72.

31. A summary of Bradford's difficulties with Philadelphia authorities appears in McMurtie, *A History of Printing in the United States*, pp. 2–9.

32. Bradford had argued the right of the jury to find the law, not merely the fact. Although Justice Jennings at first refused the point, his instructions to the jury told otherwise. In the end, the jury was unable to agree. See Nelson, "Seditious Libel in Colonial America," p. 165.

33. Botein, "'Meer Mechanics' and an Open Press," p. 174.

34. Rollo Silver, "Government Printing in Massachusetts-Bay, 1700–1750" and "Government Printing in Massachusetts, 1751–1801," *Studies in Bibliography* 16 (1963), pp. 161–200.

35. For numbers suggestive of the declining importance of government printing jobs in the Revolutionary era, see Mary Ann Yodelis, *Who Paid the Piper? Publishing Economics in Boston 1763–1775* (Lexington, KY: Association for American Journalism, 1975). See also Silver, "Government Printing in Massachusetts-Bay, 1700–1750" and "Government Printing in Massachusetts, 1751–1801."

36. Botein, "'Meer Mechanics' and an Open Press," p. 177.

37. Ibid.

38. Botein notes, "It was pointed out to Bradford that he should have known better from the experiences of his father-in-law [Andrew Sowle], who had 'suffered much in England' at the hands of a hostile government." See "'Meer Mechanics' and an Open Press," p. 175.

39. Botein also makes note of Franklin's essay in his "'Meer Mechanics' and an Open Press," p. 183.

40. As cited by M.A. Yodelis, "Boston's First Major Newspaper War: A 'Great Awakening' of Freedom," *Journalism Quarterly* (spring 1974), p. 210.

41. The line of this argument is drawn from Lawrence H. Leder, "The Role of Newspapers in Early America 'In Defense of Their Own Liberty,'" *Huntington Library Quarterly*, vol. 30, no. 1 (November 1966), pp. 1–16.

42. The "Apology" appeared in the *South Carolina Gazette*, edited by one of Franklin's partners, Thomas Whitmarsh, as a response to criticism of his decision to print material offensive to some Anglican readers. The verse version appeared in 1749 in the *Maryland Gazette* (1745–66; 1783–84; 1878), a paper edited by Jonas Green, who had been associated with Franklin in Philadelphia in the mid-1730s.

43. Franklin frequently penned letters to himself as printer and then published both letters and answers in his columns. Botein comments that Briton Aaron Hill anticipated this device when he encouraged Samuel Richardson to print opposing opinions in his *Gazetteer*. See Botein, "'Meer Mechanics' and an Open Press," p. 164. On Franklin, see McMurtie, *A History of Printing in the United States*, p. 30.

44. See Botein, "'Meer Mechanics' and an Open Press," p. 165.

45. Jürgen Habermas, *The Structural Transformation of the Public Sphere*, trans. Thomas Burger with Frederick Lawrence (Cambridge: MIT Press, 1989).

46. Many journalism historians consider "objectivity" to be a nineteenth-century invention. See Michael Schudson, *Discovering the News: A Social History of American Newspapers* (New York: Basic Books, 1978). See also David Mindich, *Building the Pyramid: A Cultural History of 'Objectivity' in American Journalism, 1832–1894* (New York: New York University Press, 1999).

47. Botein, "'Meer Mechanics' and an Open Press," p. 162.

48. Ibid., p. 189.

49. It is worthy of note that one of Franklin's earliest falsified letters to the editor was written on the subject of such "dulness" [sic] in Bradford's *Weekly Mercury*. See the *Pennsylvania Gazette*, October 1733. Cited by McMurtie, *A History of Printing in the United States*, p. 30.

50. See Lawrence W. Levine, *High Culture, Low Culture* (Cambridge: Harvard University Press, 1992).

51. Franklin, *Autobiography*, p. 159.

52. See Carol Sue Humphrey, *The Press and the Young Republic, 1783–1833* (Westport, CT: Greenwood Press, 1996).

CHAPTER 2

Audience Engagements: Marketing Early Women's Magazines and the Construction of the Popular Woman Reader

Like formal American democracy, women's magazine "democracy" required an educated, activated population to make it work. Yet the magazine was a complex form, born of and born into changing reception practices and literary mores. Printers faced inadequate reader preparation, widespread social condemnation, their own limitations in addressing unprecedented female audiences, and markedly changing times. But the idea of the American women's magazine was too promising to let go.

CHANGING MINDS: THE EMERGENT MARKET FOR AMERICAN WOMEN'S MAGAZINES

Even a white, native-born woman in the Early Republic might well have lived out her life without acquiring sufficient literacy skills to fully participate in print culture. A growing belief in the importance of universal education was spread by popular nonfiction books such as Dr. Benjamin Rush's *Thoughts on Female Education* (1787), but even Rush proposed to limit women's access to certain kinds of knowledge he and others deemed dangerous for the female mind. In a 1786 preview to his book published in Mathew Carey's renowned *Columbian Magazine* (1786–90), Rush specifically called for a ban on women's reading of novels.[1] Noah Webster was similarly liberal on the issue of women's education: he declared in his *American Magazine* in 1788 that women should learn English, arithmetic, and geography, and be less instructed in music, dancing, and drawing. But he hastened to add that women definitely should not be permitted to explore popular fiction.[2]

Whatever the aims of even the most progressive "universal education" proponents, in reality women's educational opportunities remained narrow and few in the Early Republic. At the time the first women's magazines appeared, as Cathy Davidson has written, there remained "a substantial discrepancy between the prescriptive statements on the importance of 'universal' education and the actual performance of institutions intended to achieve that goal."[3] Not all children attended school; only 12 percent of children between the ages of four and fifteen were educated at public grammar and writing schools after the passage of the first compulsory education laws, in Massachusetts, in 1789. Furthermore, Davidson points out, girls were required by law to attend school for fewer hours per day and for fewer months per year than boys. And most young girls "continued to receive their education only at dame schools or at the summer schools in which often itinerant teachers or local women taught subjects such as . . . advanced sewing and embroidery."[4]

The most dependable literacy studies available estimate that white men achieved nearly universal "literacy"—defined, at the time, as the ability to both read and sign their names—by about 1740. However, not more than 50 percent of white women could sign their names by 1790. And this figure comes from New England, a region renowned for learning and literacy at the time. In the Southern colonies, even white men probably did not attain more than about 65 percent literacy by the time the first women's magazines appeared.[5]

Women's writing was widely proscribed and policed. Some more affluent women did learn to write from private tutors, but in the main, writing remained a job-related skill and a male domain in the Early Republic.[6] A homosocial preserve, it was imparted by male teachers exclusively to male students for generations. The powerful gender exclusivity of writing can be read in the work of the few early American women who both dared and were educationally prepared to write. Their works go to extraordinary rhetorical and metaphorical lengths to justify taking up the pen.[7]

Young girls did receive a roughly equal education in reading, though, since it was thought essential for everyone for devotional reasons.[8] Still, toward the end of the eighteenth century, just as the first women's magazines appeared, established reception practices began to change, rendering that education inadequate. By about the 1790s, "intensive" reading, arguably the dominant mode in the colonies, began to be challenged by a competing style, dubbed "extensive reading" by scholars of the history of the book.[9] Intensive reading was associated with devotional texts, and implied deep, repeated readings of sacred texts or passages, for the purposes of discipline, catechism, and spiritual imitation. By contrast, "extensive" reading implied a versatile reader of diverse and varying tastes, who read more widely and willingly but less deeply, and for entertainment or enjoyment above all.

Although both reading styles coexisted for decades, extensive reading enjoyed the promotional push of the expanding literary economy and the solidifying secular-political ethos of the Early Republic. At the time of the publication of the *Ladies Magazine and Repository* in 1792, some devotional texts were "steady sellers," but the more conducive cultural, legal, technological, and institutional conditions of the time encouraged printers to diversify the range of material they produced. Studies of early American booksellers demonstrate a late-century surge in both importation and domestic publication of frontier stories, travelogues, captivity narratives, crime chronicles, and other fanciful fare keyed to what were emerging popular audiences.[10]

Extensive reading privileged the reader and the decoder over the read and the given. It prioritized sociability, creativity, and entertainment over discipline and didacticism, writer candor and reader enjoyment over authorial significance and audience obedience to the dictates of text. All of these aspects suggest its potential fit with the lifestyles and mindsets of affluent, cosmopolitan women.

And magazine printers were in an excellent position to perceive that appeal. Early Republican print businesses could not live by ink and plates alone. Newspapers and magazines were unstable ventures; bookselling was a marginal operation throughout the eighteenth century as printers struggled to get discount rates competitive with London retailers and locally printed editions remained inferior to English editions in terms of quality.[11] Consequently, early American print and bookshops were also general stores, selling a range of commodities, from spectacles and sealing wax, to domestic goods such as cloth, shoes, and food.[12] As proprietors of such social, literary, and commercial outfits, printers were especially privy to the pace of women's lives and leisure, to interests and preferences, and to the extent of their disposable means.

But cultivating the gender demographic within the larger shift to extensive would take conscientious effort. It was simply presumed that women, like the working classes, would read differently from the middle- and upper-class male norm.[13] Systematic reading was generally endorsed for young people in the late eighteenth century, but its proponents did not include women in "the people." As the eminent cultural historian Richard Altick has explained, systematic reading promised to help build good workers;[14] thus, the presumed reader of the past was clearly marked male.

Men of various class backgrounds had long ago begun the process of acclimating to varied experiences with prose and print. As Michael Warner discusses, artisans and tradesmen—the other major semiliterate groups in the Early Republic—became comfortable navigating a public realm increasingly constituted by print and the press through their exposure to "one kind of printed artifact that could have been regarded as an everyday secular object": the legal form. The "astonishing variety" of forms that emerged after about 1720 included "summonses, writs of attachment, deeds of transfer, apprentice indentures, customs receipts, surveyors' certificates, tax assessment forms, land grants, powers of attorney, military discharge, complaints for suits in equity, recognizance appeals, commissions civil and military, post-rider oaths, special warrants, bills obligatory, mortgages for slaves, . . . and more."[15] Women, however, experienced no such quotidian exposure to attune them to the new world of public print.

Until, perhaps, the women's magazine. The most ambitious printers could see before them a potentially lucrative women's market, and were determined to do everything in their power to develop it. During the 1790s, just as the first women's magazines appeared, printers also produced a rash of entertaining and instructive texts for women: they produced increasing numbers of education and advice manuals for women and upped their importation of novels, a form with gendered appeal from the start. Isaac Ralston, a Philadelphia bookseller and editor of the *Ladies Museum* (1800), spoke for the trend in the trade when he proclaimed that "a spirit of literature . . . at present prevails among noble-minded females"—and "ought to be encouraged."[16]

ENCOURAGING THE SPIRIT OF LITERATURE: OBSTACLES AND ANSWERS

To encourage that spirit, magazine producers needed new competencies, new social practices and all new cultural rationales (or controls). They had to educate their audiences to negotiate the miscellaneous magazine environment, and possibly answer its call to both read and write, all during an era of literary expansion, reaction and change. They had to find ways of ingratiating a novel and complex form to an underprepared and overprotected audience with which they had little or no experience. And if these difficulties weren't enough, they also had to overcome the magazine's social stigma, which stemmed from its range of promiscuous content and the provocative presence of fiction.

Early women's magazine content was various, irregular, and authored by amateur writers, so quite demanding to decode. The earliest examples varied in length from a single, four-page quarto monthly to some fifty-four pages weekly. Page designs varied from issue to issue as well as from periodical to periodical, but the majority of the early women's magazines were set in a one- to three-column layout. Most were packed in with tiny, six-point type—that is, type smaller than the size of this eight-point type. Printing technologies were limited, so few illustrations or even design elements broke up inside pages; only a single frontispiece woodcut or, by the end of the century, a copperplate engraving offered respite from the persistent mixture of miscellaneous content presented in close quarters and minuscule print.

Content was curtailed somewhat by gender assumptions at play in the Early Republic, yet the first women's magazines still exposed readers to an "astonishing variety" of voices and views—some of them more challenging than many would imagine. Right from the start in 1792, a reader of the *Ladies Magazine and Repository* encountered a lengthy excerpt of Mary Wollstonecraft's radical feminist tract, *Vindication of the Rights of Woman*. In its first issue, New York's *Lady's Monitor* (1801–02) carried "A Second Vindication of the Rights of Women," contributed "By an American lady . . . Never Before Published."[17] Readers of one of the earliest issues of New York's *Lady's Magazine and Musical Repository* (1801–02), too, confronted a "Plan for the Emancipation of the Fair Sex," in which an anonymous author simply accepts women's suffrage as a first step in the rise of the infant Republic. It is "necessary for the lovely claimants to petition the legislature to sanction their emancipation by law," the anonymous contributor goads.[18]

Unfamiliar perspectives on more general topics of the day were also revealed. Early women's magazines carried many of the same departments as contemporaneous general-interest magazines did, but they differed distinctly in their devotion to women's lives and minds. As David Paul Nord has written, only 11 percent of the articles or stories in one of the most successful magazines of the Early Republic, the *New-York Magazine* (1790–97), portrayed woman as a main character,[19] and these pieces addressed traditional feminine subjects, such as marriage and seduction, as well as "tales of women's heroism, calls for women's education, and articles . . . sensitive to women's concerns."[20] In contemporaneous women's magazines, virtually all contributions made women the subject of the story, and female authorship often affected the expected stance, structure and flow of a piece.

The attention to women's perspectives made the early women's magazine an intriguing but potentially disorienting place. Consider the earliest "Correspondence" columns. They presented letters from maidens to beaux, reconfiguring gender dynamics.[21] Letters from aunts to nieces also turned up, spanning extended family relations, at least within female kinship networks.[22] And letters from mothers to virtually everyone potentially subverted patriarchy.[23]

It is true that by the turn of the nineteenth century, more and more women's magazines began to exhibit some self-conscious formatting, a move emerging industrywide. Both general-interest and women's magazines also offered local community notes very early on, usually in back pages. Novels, short stories, and other literary works—genres that would join fashion copy as definitive staples of the women's magazine by 1825[24]—still took a backseat to nonfiction bits in all American magazines at the turn of the nineteenth century.[25] Contributions to most magazines, including women's magazines, typically included letters, a dominant mode; essays; travelogues; "observations" on various concepts, ideals or scenes; moral parables; and many sorts of fragments.[26]

Actually, some typical magazine formats were begun by women's magazines, although few have recognized that until now. Serialization, for example, is said to have begun with Harriet Beecher Stowe's blockbuster *Uncle Tom's Cabin*, published in *The National Era* (1847–60) between June 1851 and April 1852.[27] But a serialized novel by the amateur woman author "Anna" appeared in New York's *Weekly Magazine* (1797–98) in 1797.[28] Charles Brockden Brown's serial novel *Alciun* followed in Philadelphia's *Weekly Magazine* (1798–99) in 1798.[29] In fact, several serialized novels by amateur writers had appeared by the start of the nineteenth century. The first installment of *The Unfortunate Female*, for example, ran in the premiere issue of Samuel White's *Weekly Visitor or Ladies' Miscellany* (1802–12) in October 1802.[30]

Despite some movement toward structure and organization in early nineteenth-century magazines, "miscellaneous" still accurately describes content, including the internal content of these emerging departments and the internal quality of the vast majority of individual contributions as well. Within "fiction" departments, for example, various sorts of narratives appeared, including sentimental tales, allegories and parables, and narrated character sketches. Some magazines targeted to women, such as the four-page, $2.00/year *Boston Weekly Magazine* (1802–5) under the editorial direction of Susannah Rowson, the author of the phenomenally successful sentimental fiction *Charlotte Temple* (1792), classified letters as a variety of fiction, listing them in its table of contents in the "Novelist" department.[31]

Many submissions to early women's magazines simply confound formal identification, displaying an irregular admixture of narrative, poetry, argument, reporting, exegesis, dialogue, and didacticism within themselves.[32] Even the many short fragments published could begin as essays and end as stories, or begin as "observations" and end as parables, poems, or cautionary tales. Although the practice of anonymous or pseudonymous publication—a convention eroded by the byline policies of women's magazines of the 1830s, particularly *Godey's Lady's Book* under Sarah Hale[33]—makes it nearly impossible to designate the gender of authors with absolute certainty, one authorial dimension can be stated without hesitation: virtually all original work in early women's magazines was composed by amateur writers experimenting with print and public expression. As a result, contributions often display multiple, muddled, or ambiguous objectives and attitudes, and rhetorical shifts of surprising latitude.

Reading an early American women's magazine was therefore an exercise in versatility. These gregarious publications required women readers to interpret often incomplete stories and parables, follow multiple serials and travelogues, decipher amateur poetry, attend debates, assess advice, and fathom fragments all in the course of a single, small-print issue—and on an ongoing basis.

These issues for readers, of course, were augmented by additional problems for magazine producers. They faced the difficulties connected with bringing such demanding publications to an unprecedented and underprepared audience, and also of legitimating them in a culture that saw both their properties and their contents as tinged with transgression and compromised virtue. As Robert B. Winans has written, women's reading of fiction was considered "immoral, unrealistic and time-wasting" and the cultural opposition to it extended to the periodical press, because "magazines and newspapers were also major purveyors of the fiction being condemned."[34] "Novel reading" was considered a "Cause of Female Depravity" as one widely reprinted 1787 article put it, proclaiming "the poor deluded female imbibes erroneous principles, and from thence pursues a flagrantly vicious line of conduct."[35] As men as well as tradesmen, magazine printers could hardly have been unaware of the disrepute in which the novel—and along with it the whole prospect of women's exposure to extensive reading experiences—was held.[36]

A STIMULUS TO VIRTUE: MARKETING THE AMERICAN MAGAZINE FOR WOMEN

Printers addressed these issues by first putting their controversial publications in their best patriotic dress. Most tried what Isaac Ralston, editor of Philadelphia's *Ladies Museum* (1800), did: he veiled his project in the dress of the Republican values most consistent with the civic ideals prevailing in secular, urbane Philadelphia at the time. To appease those who deplored women's wide reading for stoking their passions and leading them astray, Ralston aligns himself with a didactic literature that "sought to substitute civic virtue for passion," claiming that women's popular reading is actually a step in the right direction.[37] Reading his women's magazine, he maintains, will lead not to ruin but to its nation-building opposites, knowledge and virtue—at least if taken in the proper doses. (We will discuss these dosage requirements shortly.) Ralston explains that "latent genius" is first "roused by reading, with the utmost avidity, and with the least discrimination, such books, as most interested their hearts, or imaginations."[38] To his mind, "every stimulus to knowledge, is a tribute to virtue."[39]

John Heard, the Philadelphia editor of the *Ladies Monitor* (1801–3), offers a more market-attuned version of Ralston's basic approach. He couches the magazine's identity in the language of democratic diversity while also allowing the underlying promise of reader pleasure to break through the surface of his language. "Variety will be our first consideration, so persons of different views and opinions . . . should be gratified," he writes.[40]

Subsequent women's magazine producers similarly draped their projects in some kind of respectable Republican garb, masking in this all-American appeal the titillating promises of reader pleasure. The editor of Philadelphia's *Ladies' Literary Museum; or, Weekly Repository* (1817–19) shifts a bit, pushing past topical content and social context into a more intimate field. He moves to sell his magazine by the mood and emotional experience it offers. His "varied selections extend from grave to gay, from witty to severe."[41]

Male editors were able to produce fairly effective marketing for the early women's magazines in part because promotional pitches were addressed to other men. Their visions and voices were less assured when selling to their women readers directly. Women's magazine editors struggled for nearly two decades to grasp the right modes of address for their readers, in the process constructing some unanticipated possibilities for women at the very launch of the tradition.

William Gibbons, the editor of the first women's magazine, sticks to the tried and true. He adopts a conventional eighteenth-century pose in his one-page preface to the *Ladies Magazine and Repository*. At the outset, the printer positions himself in the masculine role of solicitous or Petrarchan lover, proposing to women readers that his periodical should become the offspring of the union of editor and readers. He promises "to lay at [women's] feet the first fruits of our literary labors, that they may smile upon them, and cherished by their smiles, grow up into ripened maturity."[42]

Gibbons uses conventional gendered address in speaking to his incipient female audience. He calls on women's presumed vanity and always-immanent maternity to make his case. But this doesn't seem to be enough. Soon he begins wildly pitching with every line he can think of, construing women variously, rather than consecutively, as sentimental maidens and mothers, wives and dutiful daughters, sisters and seducible mistresses. His obsequious flattery and sticky-sweet literary language also splits his vision in another way, rendering readers in social and mythical dimensions at the same time.

Subsequent printers similarly deployed gendered, multiple address—and raised similar problems and possibilities. Some twenty years later, the 1817 preface to H.C. Lewis's *Ladies' Literary Museum* moves among different but a no less contradictory collection of conventionally gendered roles. Lewis's nineteenth-century pitch addresses women's presumed pity and sympathy, emotional qualities derived of their social roles as mothers and wives. He repeatedly stresses that he has been "at length reduced, by a succession of recent misfortunes and disappointments, to appeal openly, as his last resource, to the *benevolence* of the public." He pleads "poverty and distress," and "*Necessity*, the most absolute—*Necessity* . . . is the sole cause that compels him to set aside that natural delicacy of pride, and throw off the disguise ever worn by mankind to conceal the real situation of pecuniary embarrassments, and to solicit, thus candidly solicit support from the public, A RELIEF AND SUPPORT FOR HIMSELF, HIS WIFE, AND HIS CHILDREN."[43]

But Lewis's appeal to the hearts of women is soon supplemented—and somewhat contradicted—by another voice. At the end of his first quarter, Lewis prints a new pitch, which downplays feminine benevolence and instead appeals to the competitive instincts and self-interest of the "Ladies of Philadelphia." Ostensibly written by "Ellen," the second attempt entreats women not to let the magazine fold because "it would be a censure on all those to whom [the editor] *chiefly* looks for the patronage of this and the *only* paper of the kind in Philadelphia—*the Ladies!*" Ladies of Philadelphia," the writer continues, "what say you? Shall this useful paper, *the only one devoted so chiefly to ourselves*, be seen no more, by withdrawing your mite [sic]?" "Ladies, *for the sake of ourselves*," the writer concludes in a rousing finale, "let us nourish our own offspring to a good old age.—The gentlemen of Philadelphia support upwards of a *dozen* periodicals papers for *their* use and amusement . . . and who would like to have it said, that *the Ladies* refuse to maintain *one for their's?*—**the LADIES!**"[44]

These American men joined a long list of printers on both sides of the Atlantic who used multiple visions of femininity to address women. Kathryn Shevelow has argued that multiple, gendered address in British periodicals for women effectively established a framework for confining and subjecting women to the paternal authority of male magazine makers. Borrowing the modes and manners of the paternal advice book, Shevelow argues, "the covert rhetorical effect" of multiple gendered address "carries a message of female subordination in patriarchal culture."[45]

In early American women's magazines, however, multiple address may have functioned differently. Although Shevelow rightly points out the deployment of traditional gender roles in early magazines for women, the effects of such ad hoc discursive concoctions may have been to suggest more fluid and changeable understandings of gender identity. Given the more active role demanded of early American magazine readers, it is plausible that a female reader's exposure to myriad representations, self-representations, and perspectives might at least alert her to the myriad ways in which she, as an individual subject, could be construed—or could come to construe herself. Gendered though the earliest editors' come-ons are, they also explode monolithic notions of femininity, and their garbled presentation only enhanced the potentially serviceable friction between divergent or competing ideas. Multiple address, especially when mixed (or mixed up) as it often was in early American magazines, could unmask some constructions of gender and undercut the male authority on which they depend. It could be more generative than singular or uniform address, or than no address at all.

Such conflicts of interest pervaded printers' efforts to market the first women's magazines. They were forced to negotiate opposing sets of interests when it came to magazine reading and the ongoing exchange of ideas as well. To control the promiscuous possibilities and expressive potential of the magazine (without reducing their potential as a draw to readers), early magazine publishers began issuing new rules for women's reading styles and expressive etiquette. Most shared the same first move: they displaced the public powers of the magazine onto a private, domestic space. The emergent metaphor for the American women's magazine would not be the democratic forum or even the marketplace bazaar, but the middle-class parlor. This marketing image made magazine expression and exchange appear as fashionable (presumably to subscribers) as highbrow socializing, and as practically harmless (to male cultural authorities) as women's chitchat. The *Ladies' Monitor*, like many of its contemporaries, imaged itself as "an agreeable companion to fair readers" and its interactive dynamics as "a vehicle for communications of such lucubrations as opportunity may enable them to bestow."[46]

The parlor metaphor ingeniously instituted controls over magazine readers and reading. It served to contain women's agency within patriarchy-attuned ideas of female propriety, all the while seeming to offer women control and command of standards and practices. The image packaged restrictive standards of speech and behavior as an advantageous social opportunity (thus raising the desirability of magazine subscription and participation), while appearing to give women self-rule (thus at least nodding to the democratic promises and potential of the magazine form without granting any risky rights).

But like multiple gendered address, the scheme partly backfired. The American women's magazine remained a form of public space that people noticed, and the parlor image rallied women's collective feeling and actions there. The parlor context actually promoted women's collective work by first covering some critical lapses in educational preparation, social status, and confidence. As a place of conversation and encounter rather than writing and reading, the parlor allowed the women's magazine to image all participation as oral. As a result, the magazine's connections to the un-feminine act of writing were effaced, perhaps encouraging those women who could write to contribute and those with little experience or self-confidence to give it a try. And the oral nature of parlor interaction also evaded social disparities between those women who could only read and those who could also write. It thereby helped unify readers and writers, ostensibly, into a stronger sisterhood.

And that sisterhood would indeed be powerful. The parlor's ethos of mutually supportive conversation and exchange was already suffused with a strong sense of gender authority. Inherited British standards helped upscale women's magazine readers to understand the parlor as a feminine space in which women rightfully ruled, setting the agenda and standards. It accorded participating ladies (though not their servants, of course) superior status and self-government skills over the fathers, husbands, and brothers of the world. As an anonymous contributor to the *Lady and Gentleman's Pocket Magazine of Literature and Polite Amusement* (1796) put it, "One month with a well bred and amiable lady is of more use . . . than a year with some of the best male preceptors."[47]

Plus, for magazine communities, all women present had been invited and were welcome. They all belonged. Indeed, the parlor proposed that all women who opened the magazine were not merely invited, but were instantly elevated to the level of lady of the house. Thus, a community of equals was created and sustained, and each participating women felt especially empowered—even called upon—to speak, to organize, to entertain, to lead.

"Hints on Conversation," an anonymous May 28, 1803, contribution to the *Boston Weekly Magazine* under Susannah Rowson, reveals the governing values of parlorlike magazine encounters. Rule one: unity in community is central. One "should never whisper or share secrets with those nearby," the *Weekly*'s writer admonishes; "it divides the group."[48] As Patricia Okker argues, a marked emphasis on exchange within a context of trusting togetherness became a definitive quality of the women's magazine of the nineteenth century.[49] Moreover, she says, community among readers, writers, and editors helped sustain ensuing social and political moves.[50]

More nuances of women's magazine community are revealed by the 1801 preface to New York's *Ladies' Monitor*. Notably, the *Monitor*'s editor begins by writing that he will not exclude discussion of such arguably masculine subjects as "news for the politician," "chemistry," "nondescripts" "for the naturalist," and "aerial and CALORIC speculations" for "the chemist."[51] However, he will exclude anything violent, deceitful, or divisive from the magazine.

We shall not occupy our pages with details of battles or sieges; or murders, by the sword, or by famine . . . with accounts of usurpations of governments by ambitious demagogues, or the destruction of monarchs by their own intrigues, or the craft and 'skill' of ministers," the editor begins. "We shall not give a weekly detail of duels (of Congress-men or others), . . . of the various forms of challenges, the names of seconds, or the length of the pistols of the duelists.[52]

Furthermore, its editor notes, "no advertisements shall be admitted into THE LADY'S MONITOR," suggesting as many later and even contemporary commentators have done, that advertising in women's magazines is a male invention that has had mainly detrimental effects on its female reader-consumers. By offering an extensive range of subject matter in a climate cleansed of division, early magazine marketing at once kowtows to ideas about feminine frailty and weakness and offers an empowering opportunity for collective engagement with the wide range of information and knowledge at hand.

ENGAGE OFTEN, BUT NOT LONG: CONSTRUCTING
THE POPULAR WOMAN READER

Not all printers held exactly the same disposition toward their readers, of course, or toward what should be permitted.[53] But surprising agreement occurred across more than a decade of writing about one point of convergence between parlor conversation and the magazine-reading process. A *Boston Weekly Magazine* contributor says it simply, stressing that in parlor conversation, one should talk "often, but not long."[54]

This simple principle formed the core of a methodology for women's right reading that quickly took shape in the early magazines. Time and again, contributors and printers called for the consistent reading of a wide range of text types, regulated by short exposure and episodic attention. This paradigm clearly responded to the demand for reader versatility as well as to disparaging assumptions about women's intellects. But mainly, it served the most practical interests of magazine producers: consistent but episodic reading constructed the popular woman reader as the ideal reader of the women's magazine, with its miscellaneous contents and serial format.

The first formal instruction in women's reading ever published in an American women's magazine is "Hints on Reading," a March 1793 contribution to Gibbons's *Ladies Magazine and Repository*. An anonymous writer counsels that "Reading—to be useful—should be regular—[just as] the most instructive conversation is regular."[55] The writer develops the analogy between women's right reading and both schooling and parlor conversation, explaining that "Some books are to be read once, and some always to be read, just as we find some persons in the world whose company we never wish to be in a second time, and others whom we wish to be with often, and always, if it were possible."

The writer nicely maneuvers the seismic shift occurring in reading practice in the Early Republic. Both intensive, repeated reading and extensive, diverse reading are integrated in the recommendations here. The inclusion of both of these competing styles reflects the moment of transition within which the American women's magazine emerged, but also speaks to the pivotal place that women readers occupied in the earliest conceptions of a rising popular reading audience. Women were not the only readers encouraged to master and maintain both intensive and extensive styles. The episodic style developed for them would also be recommended for another emergent audience with enormous future potential: children.[56]

Whatever didactic intentions are revealed in tone here, even this writer allows that choices within the expanding marketplace rests with women readers themselves. Many early magazine contributions attempted to advise women on making and managing decisions about what to read repeatedly and reverently (in the intensive style), and what to peruse more lightly for interest and entertainment (in the extensive mode). Ultimately, though, all contributions concluded on the same note as this first one does: a good woman reader never fails to consult her own best judgment. "In reading your deep, grave and learned authors," the *Ladies Magazine and Repository* writer admonishes, "it is necessary to make many a pause, and consider how far what he says concords with your own opinions and experience, for [they] are very apt to lead you astray, because you adopt their conclusion without examining their arguments."[57]

As this lesson instructs, right reading practices ought to be episodic, ongoing, and as personal as a conversation with a trusted friend. This approach is a virtual prototype for the episodic reading, and viewing, now often seen as inescapably gendered. The origin of episodic reading here in the first popular gendered genre in the United States explains why such episodic reading would have become so preponderant a model of women's reception. Yet, its effect on women's relationship to texts and to making meanings is far less clear. In this instance, readers are encouraged to incorporate regular reading into the personal and quotidian rhythms of their lives; they are also counseled to do so critically and self-reflectively, keeping their own views and good judgment in the center of their minds. As a result, the "hints" may arise from a host of other concerns, but the explicit counsel of this contribution instigates critical interpretations of written texts. The personally attuned reading endorsed here gives a woman "pause" to consider the extent to which written contents "concord" with her intellect, her experiences, and her convictions.

The author of "The Good Effects of Bad Novels," an original essay by "E.A.," published in the debut issue of the *Ladies' Magazine and Musical Repository* (1801–2) in January 1801, is another of the earliest contributions to recommend what amounts to episodic reading for women. This writer's comments, too, suggest potentially empowering outcomes he might not have intended. Despite the title, E.A. seems to be talking about magazine reading as much as novel reading: "It is the *Spectator*, I think, who remarks that in order to allure persons to a habit of reading, it is only necessary that they should read a little, frequently," the writer begins, "and that if they do this, he cares not whether the subject be 'Tom Thumb' or 'Thomas Aquinas'—gross nonsense, or profound argument." Like many proponents of the popular presses to come,[58] E.A. argues that those who read the first in the prescribed style "will in time, wish to study the second."[59]

A subsequent contribution, titled "The Method of Reading for Female Improvement," was also published in the *Ladies' Magazine and Musical Repository*, this time in the March 1801 issue. The apparently male author, I. Schomberg, wishes that "the female part of human creation, on whom Nature has poured out so many charms with so lavish a hand, would pay some regard to the cultivation of their understanding." Schomberg says this cultivation can be "easily accomplished," and toward that end he offers a method of women's reading that echoes guidelines published in women's magazines during the past decade. Like earlier interested parties, Schomberg's program for women's reading depends on a rhythm of concentrated attention to certain texts, undertaken in short, episodic stints: "The first rule to be laid down to anyone who reads to improve," he begins, "is never to read but with attention. As the abstruse parts of learning are not necessary to the accomplishment of one of your sex," he immediately adds, "a small degree of it will suffice."[60]

But, he adds, these short stints should be repeated, time and again, to be truly useful for imitation, the goal of the intensive style, and personal growth, the more social (and commercial) goal of the extensive one. Schomberg, like other magazine editors before and after him, sees women's reading as akin to productive and pleasant conversation when he explains that

There are none in our language more useful and entertaining than the *Spectators*, *Tatlers* and *Guardians*. They are the standards of the English tongue, and as such should be read over and over again; for as we imperceptibly slide into the manners and habits of those persons with whom we most frequently converse, so reading being, as it were, a silent conversation, we insensibly write and talk in the style of the authors we have the most often read, and who have left the deepest impressions on our minds.[61]

Some scholars have seen gendered reading and viewing as empowering to women's subjectivity and styles of agency,[62] whereas others argue that it entraps and disables them by undermining the capacity for criticism and resistance.[63] This divide about readers rehearses the larger debate about the effect of women's magazines at play today. Exploring this paradigm at its origin offers some evidence that it performed enabling functions for women readers early on. Episodic reading did through context what legal forms had done through content for new groups of male readers: it familiarized new kinds of textual practices and relations to women by keying reception to their quotidian rhythms and individual needs. At the same time, it mediated between conservative ideas of women readers as easily absorbed and led astray by popular print—an underlying premise of intensive reading—and the emergent notion needed by the Early Republican literary marketplace that women were a prime group who should be ready, willing, and able to choose and use popular literary fare. Integrating the two modes, all in a context that recognized gendered lives and expectations, kept women on the stage—even in the spotlight—as the public realm grew increasingly constituted by prose, print, and the press.

Although the premises for many of these special reading practices for women patronized gendered limitations in women's intellect and reading capacity, they also evinced and even encouraged some subversive opportunities. In both precept and practice, these magazine articles teach their women readers to examine arguments before agreeing (or disagreeing) with their apparent intentions, to contend with conventional wisdom, and to create or complete narratives that bespeak their own experiences and convictions. This construction invites women readers to use the lapsed time and the intellectual space between episodic readings—a rhythmic approach echoed and emphasized by the monthly publication of magazines—to construct their own meanings. Such advice, particularly when coupled with what historian Nancy Cott calls the "functional ambiguity" of early discourse about women's cultural roles—an ambiguity only exaggerated by the miscellaneous conditions and amateur authorship that made up early women's magazine content—together facilitated the "active" and/or "resistive" reading now celebrated as a means of liberation and empowerment for women and other marginalized groups.[64] Indeed, such critical decoding skills lie at the heart of media literacy movements designed to fight the dominating potential of television, film, and other mass media today.[65] The (potentially large) gap between initial idea and elaborated ideology in amateur writing, the (also potentially large) space between episodic reading, punctuated by women's consultation with their own perceptions, beliefs, and experiences, could, and here *should*, be filled or resolved by the reader herself. This woman reader remains "feminine" through setting and values and address, but is neither passive nor an easy dupe of destructive intentions. She is the agile, able, self-aware reader who has, by modern standards, all the abilities she needs to emancipate herself from domination or misrepresentation in discourse.[66]

A composite sketch of the ideal popular woman reader is drawn by "G. Keate, Esquire" in a contribution to the *Lady and Gentleman's Pocket Maga-*

zine of Literature and Polite Amusement (1796). Keate observes a variety of available reading styles and evaluates their implications for personality development and social improvement. His equation between reading and thinking, reception style and self, supports an underlying conceptualization of the intimate relationship between rhetoric and reality so promising for future women's magazine contributors.

Keate playfully describes six reader types: "Superficial Reader," "Idle Reader," "Sleepy Reader," "Peevish Reader," "Candid Reader," and "Conjectural Reader." From this list, Sleepy can be dropped from consideration since Keate himself rather dismisses him as "a sleepy man of dull languid and soporific temperament" whose bookshelves are filled with "no works of genius" but instead with "plenty of soporific treatises, under varied titles of Journals, Annotations, books of controversy, and Metaphysical Dissertations."[67]

Through the evaluation of the remaining five reader typologies, a blueprint of the ideal women's magazine reader emerges. The Superficial Reader, while carrying a derogatory label, is the ideal consumer of periodicals. "He contents himself with abstracts from newspapers, magazines, and reviews," Keate asserts.[68] However, this reader is hardly lazy, or lacking in method or purpose. The presence of such qualities becomes apparent in the description of the Idle Reader, who is next discussed as "the reverse" of the Superficial Reader. The Idle Reader, by contrast, "is a great purser [sic] of little volumes, but reads without method, or pursuit, not making knowledge, but amusement his object," Keate writes.

Even superficial magazine readers—perhaps, even *especially* those readers—need mechanisms or qualities to read for the pursuit of instructive knowledge. The Peevish Reader, who comes next, is quickly explained away as "an object of compassion" because he is defined by Keate as "finding the highest satisfaction in discovering fault," and "in the imperfect state of humane labors, he must pass his time very miserably."[69] (Soon women contributors will explicitly define this sort of reader, "made up of conceit and ill humour, [who] cavils with the design, the coloring, or the finishing of every piece that comes before him," as a clear masculine type.[70]) To "counterpose his spleen," the author offers descriptions of the Candid and the Conjectural readers, thus suggesting strongly that they remain the desirable types.

And these two types validate the vision of reader agency and creativity also elaborated elsewhere in women's magazines of this period. Although evoked using the masculine pronoun, the Candid Reader has some arguably "feminine" qualities: not only is this image created in and for a women's magazine, but also the Candid Reader is an "amiable spirit" who is "slow to censure; eager to applaud." "Convinced by what arduous steps, superior excellence is attained, his [or her] liberal mind cherishes every effort of genius, and unwillingly condemns what . . . correct judgment cannot approve."[71]

The Conjectural Reader is the final image Keate presents. This reader is a creative one, who, as other contributors have asserted that a woman reader should, fills in the gaps between what learned authors propose and what she understands from previous lessons, experience, or personal conviction. The Conjectural Reader "exercises his ingenuity . . . by clearing up passages he supposes [writers] left obscure, and interpreting them by his own conceptions; discovering beauties where the author perhaps intended none, and tracing out meanings he never had in view."

When all is said and done, what kind of reader is construed? First, the ideal woman reader is a "superficial" reader, a perhaps unnecessarily derogatory moniker for one whose agility and wide interests enable her to move avidly and easily through the magazine's extensive range of reading material. Second, she should be "candid"—that is, unpretentious, open, and also intimately engaged enough to decide the merits of whatever messages she encounters. This reader might question the values or insinuations of a text, or might even resist or reject it as false or damaging to her. Finally, she is a "conjectural" reader, who should be creative enough to interpret or complete printed text that is "obscure" or to write new meanings—including some the author never intended or had in view. This reader is an adept collaborator in the maker of meanings, for whom entertaining and instructive knowledges are determined through the exercise of her "ingenuity" and judgment.

Since the American magazine is a mildly mediated, miscellaneous collection of contrasting ideas, and its proper reading is an episodic process punctuated by personal consideration, completion, or contradiction, women's participation might well open, rather than "foreclose . . . the possibility of empirical variation and heterogeneity within actual women's responses."[72] "Contingent upon specific—and often contradictory—textual mechanisms and operations on the one hand, and upon active and productive part played by female audiences in constructing textual meanings . . . on the other," the early American women's magazine could excite immanent possibilities for female intellection, authority, self-awareness, and voice.[73]

This is precisely the point that the formalist theorist M.M. Bakhtin, among others, points to when arguing the liberatory operations of the novel—as long as it is read right. The active reader of the discursively diverse novel is given the opportunity to "acquire ideologies and linguistic initiative necessary to change the nature of his [or her] own image."[74]

The women's magazine is decidedly not the novel. Indeed, it must be read as a genre of its own. Nevertheless, Bakhtin's vision of audience agency very well applies to the American magazine. Perhaps the epitomizing literary form of the emerging American democracy, the magazine has always been noisier and more diverse than other texts. It incorporates both political and commercial impulses, entertaining a range of experiences, values, and social uses, and potentially developing these in unexpected directions. Through its miscellaneous variety of genres, discourses, modes of address, and reader relations, the magazine—more graphically than the novel—compels textual negotiation and critical response. The acquisition of "linguistic initiative" was, in fact, championed by the American magazine, whose "democracy" of form, diverse discursive practices, and requirement of an actively engaged readership distinguished it from its British forefathers—and would do anything but "forget the ladies."[75]

NOTES

1. Cited in Frank Luther Mott, *A History of American Magazines, Vol. 1: 1741–1850* (New York: D. Appleton and Company, 1930), p. 64.

2. Noah Webster, *American Magazine*, May 1788, pp. 368–9. Cited in Mott, *A History of American Magazines, Vol. 1*, p. 64.

3. Cathy Davidson, *Revolution and the Word: The Rise of the Novel in America* (New York: Oxford University Press, 1986), p. 64.

4. Ibid.

5. The statistics are cited by Michael Warner in *Letters of the Republic: Publication and the Public Sphere in Eighteenth Century America* (Cambridge: Harvard University Press, 1990), p. 14. See also Carl F. Kaestle's summary in "The History of Literacy and the History of Readers," *Review of Research in Education*, vol. 12, pp. 11–53.

6. E. Jennifer Monaghan, "Literacy Instruction and Gender in Colonial New England," *American Quarterly*, vol. 40, no. 1 (March 1988), p. 24.

7. Michael Warner notes the analysis of Susan Gubar and others regarding the difficulties in taking up the pen that early American women wrote into their works. See Warner, *Letters of the Republic*, p. 15. See also Allison Giffen's discussion of early American women poets who, she argues, used mourning over dead children as a means of justifying their taking up the pen in "The Poetics of Loss: American Women Poets and the Elegiac Voice" (Ph.D. diss., Columbia University, 1995).

8. Monaghan, "Literacy Instruction and Gender in Colonial New England," p. 20.

9. See David D. Brown, "From Cohesion to Competition," *Printing and Society in Early America* (Worcester, MA: American Antiquarian Society, 1983).

10. See Cynthia Z. Stiverson and Gregory Stiverson, "The Colonial Retail Book Trade: Availability and Affordability of Reading Material in Mid-Eighteenth-Century Virginia," in Joyce, Hall, Brown, and Heinrich, eds., *Printing and Society in Early America* (Worcester, MA: American Antiquarian Society, 1983). See also David Paul Nord, "A Republican Literature: Magazine Reading and Readers in Late-Eighteenth Century New York," *American Quarterly*, vol. 40, no. 2 (June 1988), pp. 42–63; and Robert B. Winans, "The Growth of a Novel-Reading Public in Late Eighteenth-Century America," *Early American Literature*, vol. 9 (1975), pp. 32–45.

11. See Peter J. Parker, "The Philadelphia Printer: A Study of an Eighteenth-Century Businessman," *Business History Review*, vol. 40, no. 1 (1966), p. 26. See also Stephen Botein, "The Anglo-American Book Trade Before 1776: Personnel and Strategies"; and Cynthia Z. Stiverson and Gergory Stiverson, "The Colonial Retail Book Trade: Availability and Affordability of Reading Material in Mid-Eighteenth-Century Virginia." Both in *Printing and Society in Early America* (Worcester, MA: American Antiquarian Society, 1983).

12. Parker, "The Philadelphia Printer: A Study of an Eighteenth-Century Businessman," p. 26.

13. Margaret Beetham notes that the working class was also "assumed to read differently from the middle-class male norm" and that there was "much anxiety over appropriate reading matter" for both them and for women." See Beetham, *A Magazine of Her Own? Domesticity and Desire in the Woman's Magazine 1800–1914* (London: Routledge 1996), p. 10.

14. Richard Altick notes that systematic reading was typically pointed out in the pages of eighteenth-century British magazines, and argues that this was a way of escaping censure by the evangelicals and utilitarians who decried the "random reading for pleasure" on which the magazine clearly depended. See Altick, *The English Common Reader: A Social History of the Mass Reading Public 1800–1900* (Chicago: University of Chicago Press, 1957). The construction of the male reader as a systematic worker also reflects the rise of marketplace masculinity. See Michael Kimmel, *Manhood in America: A Cultural History* (New York: The Free Press, 1996).

15. Warner, *Letters of the Republic*, p. 18.

16. Cathy Davidson traces the "vogue in self-improvement books, ranging from reading and writing manuals (including dictionaries, primers, readers, and penmanship books)" into the nineteenth century. See *Revolution and the Word: The Rise of the Novel in America*, pp. 15–37.

17. *Ladies' Monitor*, August 15, 1801, pp. 19–20.

18. *Lady's Magazine and Musical Repository*, January 1802, pp. 43–4.

19. David Paul Nord, "A Republican Literature: A Study of Magazine Reading and Readers in Late Eighteenth-Century New York," *American Quarterly*, vol. 40, no. 2 (June 1988), p. 55.

20. Ibid.

21. See, for example, "From a Lady to Her Seducer," in the *Ladies Weekly Visitor*, April 1807, pp. 86–7, which is treated in chapter 3 herein.

22. *Weekly Visitor, or Ladies Miscellany* of December 17, 1803, p. 5. Elaine Showalter touches on the aunt-niece knowledge connection in her essay "Piecing and Writing," in Nancy K. Miller, ed. *The Poetics of Gender* (New York: Columbia University Press, 1986), p. 233.

23. See, for example, "Letters from a Mother" in the *(American) Ladies' Magazine*, April–July 1828, pp. 166–9, 221–3, 324–6.

24. Mott, *A History of American Magazines, Vol. 1*, p. 174.

25. Mott notes that "fiction gained as a magazine material" after 1794. See *A History of American Magazines, Vol. 1*, pp. 173–4.

26. Ibid., p. 174.

27. Michael Lund, *America's Continuing Story: An Introduction to Serial Fiction, 1850–1900* (Detroit: Wayne State University Press, 1993), p. 16.

28. Cited in Mott, *A History of American Magazines, Vol. 1*, p. 174.

29. Ibid.

30. *The Unfortunate Female* is anonymously published in the *Weekly Visitor or Ladies' Miscellany*, and clipped "From a late periodical work." It begins in vol. 1, no. 1 (October 1802), p. 1. An early original serialized novel, *Magnanimity: An Original Novel*, appears in the *Ladies' Literary Cabinet*, vol. 1, no. 1 (May 1819). Poet Samuel Woodworth, the magazine's editor, remains a trendsetter in early American literary culture, going on to publish the influential *New York Mirror* (1823–43), the arch rival of the *Saturday Evening Post*, and "a prime factor in creating and sustaining the Knickerbocker literary school." See John Tebbel and Mary Ellen Zuckerman, *The Magazine in America 1741–1990* (New York: Oxford University Press, 1990), pp. 9–10.

31. *Boston Weekly Magazine*, Index to Volume One (1802), p. vi.

32. Elaine Showalter discusses this tendency in women's writing in "Piecing and Writing," in Nancy K. Miller, ed., *The Poetics of Gender*, pp. 222–47.

33. See Patricia Okker, *Our Sister Editors: Sarah J. Hale and the Tradition of Nineteenth-Century American Women Editors* (Athens: University of Georgia Press, 1995), p. 90.

34. Winans finds that "the increasing quantity and shrillness of the 'public' opposition to novel-reading late in the century was apparently in direct proportion to the increasing indulgence in the practice." By the 1780s and 1790s—the era in which the women's magazine arose—"the amount of fiction printed in the magazines far outweighed the number of essays denouncing it." Robert B. Winans, "The Growth of a Novel-Reading Public in Late-Eighteenth-Century America," *Early American Literature*, vol. 9 (1975), p. 267.

35. The article is quoted in Mott, *A History of American Magazines, Vol. 1*, p. 174.

36. This issue is the subject of Davidson, *Revolution and the Word*.

37. Kerber, *Women of the Republic: Intellect and Ideology in Revolutionary America* (Chapel Hill, NC: University of North Carolina Press, 1980), p. 245.

38. *Ladies Museum*, February 25, 1800, p. 1.

39. *Ladies' Monitor*, July 15, 1801, p. 3.

40. *Ladies' Monitor*, October 10, 1801, p. 73.

41. *Ladies' Literary Museum; or, Weekly Repository* July 5, 1817, p. 1.

42. *Ladies Magazine and Repository of Entertaining and Instructive Knowledge*, August 1792. (No page numbers given.)

43. *Ladies' Literary Museum; or, Weekly Repository*, July 5, 1817, p. 1.

44. *Ladies' Literary Museum*, September 1817, p. 3.

45. Kathryn Shevelow, "Fathers and Daughters: Women as Readers of *The Tatler*," in Flynn and Schweikart, eds., *Gender and Reading*, pp. 107–23.

46. *Ladies' Monitor*, October 10, 1801, p. 73.

47. Quoted in Betha-Monica Stearns, "Before *Godey's*," *American Literature* 2 (1930), p. 250.

48. *Boston Weekly Magazine*, May 28, 1803, p. 125.

49. See Okker, *Our Sister Editors*.

50. Ibid.

51. *Ladies' Monitor*, October 10, 1801, p. 73.

52. Ibid., p. 74.

53. Ebenezer French writes that in his *Ladies Visitor* (1806–7), for example, his pages will be "open to everything which is entertaining or instructing—but closed against Politics and Obscenity." See *The Ladies Visitor*, December 4, 1806, p. 3.

54. *Boston Weekly Magazine*, May 28, 1803, p. 125.

55. D., "Hints on Reading," the *Ladies Magazine and Repository of Entertaining and Instructive Knowledge*," March 1793, pp. 171–3. A letter written as early as March 10, 1785, but printed by Gibbons in the *Ladies Magazine and Repository* in October 1792 suggests this methodology for women's reading. In "Letters from a Brother to a Sister at Boarding School," to be treated in detail in the next chapter, the usually unspecific brother is clear that his sister "should make it a general rule, never to employ [her] thoughts long on any subject, unless the contemplation of it promise to be productive of some advantage." This letter appears in the *Ladies Magazine and Repository*, October 1792, p. 62–3.

56. More research is needed in this area, but the line can be gleaned from discussions of children's books and reading in such sources as Gillian Avery, *Behold the Child: American Children and Their Books, 1621–1922* (Baltimore: Johns Hopkins University Press, 1994), Kirsten Drotner, *English Children and Their Magazines, 1751–1945* (New Haven: Yale University Press, 1988), and Gretchen Galbraith, *Reading Lives: Reconstructing Childhood, Books and Schools in Britain* (New York: St. Martin's, 1977).

57. *Ladies Magazine and Repository of Entertaining and Instructive Knowledge*, March 1793, p. 172.

58. Joseph Pulitzer explained his publication of sensational, emotion-grabbing copy and arresting illustrations in his *New York World* as a mechanism to draw

readers into his more serious news reporting and editorial pages within the paper. See Emery, Michael and Edwin Emery, *The Press and America: An Interpretive History of Mass Media* (Boston: Allyn & Bacon, 1996), pp. 177–8.

59. *Ladies' Magazine and Musical Repository*, January 1801, pp. 6–11.

60. Ibid., March 1801, p. 163.

61. Ibid., pp. 163–4.

62. See, for example, John Fiske, "Gendered Television: Femininity," in Gail Dines and Jean M. Humez, eds., *Gender, Race and Class in Media* (Thousand Oaks, CA: Sage, 1995). See also Ien Ang and Joke Hermes, "Gender and/in Media Consumption," in James Curren and Michael Gurevitch, eds. *Mass Media and Society* (New York: Edward Arnold, 1991).

63. See, for example, Deborah Rogers, "Daze of Our Lives: The Soap Opera as Feminine Text," in Gail Dines and Jean M. Humez, eds., *Gender, Race and Class in Media*. See also Tanya Modleski's explanation of soap opera viewers' unconscious resentment at being "constituted as an egoless receptacle for the suffering of others." In "The Search for Tomorrow in Today's Soap Operas," *Loving with a Vengeance: Mass-Produced Fantasies for Women* (Hamden, CT: Shoestring Press, 1982).

64. Nancy Cott, *The Grounding of Modern Feminism* (New Haven: Yale University Press, 1987), p. 20.

65. This is a dominant approach among activists in today's media literacy movement, which spans issues in the viewing of television, film, and the Internet. A good, brief overview is Richard Taylor, "Media 101," *Content*, July/August 1998, pp. 78–9.

66. Active reading is supported by a long line of scholarship, in disciplines ranging from literary studies, to media and mass communications, to psychology, to sociology. In literary study, see Flynn and Schweikart, eds., *Gender and Reading*. In media studies, several key articles can be found in Robert K. Avery and David Eason, eds., *Critical Perspectives on Media and Society* (New York: Guilford Press, 1991). In that volume, Michael Schudson provides a useful summary of the "long line of psychological research on selective attention and selective perception" in his essay, "The New Validation of Popular Culture: Sense and Sentimentality in Academia," pp. 49–68.

67. *Lady and Gentleman's Pocket Magazine of Literature and Polite Amusement*, p. 232.

68. Ibid., p. 231.

69. Ibid., p. 233.

70. "A male critic," Hale wrote in the *Ladies' Magazine* in November 1828, was prone to "criticise [sic] on style, or cut up books with the keen dissecting knife of ridicule, or triumph in the superior wit or argument, . . . or to 'deal damnation' on the dull." Such behavior, she continues, did not "accord with the province of women." See Okker, *Our Sister Editors*, pp. 47–8. See also chapter 3 herein.

71. *Lady and Gentleman's Pocket Magazine of Literature and Polite Amusement*, p. 233.

72. Ien Ang and Joke Hermes, "Gender and/in Media Consumption." In Curren and Gurevitch, eds., *Mass Media and Society*, p. 311.

73. Ibid.

74. M.M. Bakhtin, *The Dialogic Imagination* (Austin: University of Texas Press, 1981), p. 345.

75. Just two months before the Declaration of Independence was signed, Abigail Adams wrote to her husband, John, that "I cannot say that I think you are very generous to the ladies, for whilst you are proclaiming peace and good will to men, emancipating all nations, you insist upon retaining an absolute power over wives." Her comments are cited in William Bowditch, "Woman Suffrage a Right, Not a Privilege," Schlesinger Library, May-Goddard Papers, Cambridge, MA, 1879.

CHAPTER 3

Sons of Liberty and Their Silenced Sisters: Rising to Self-Representation in the Women's Magazines of the Early Republic

The *Ladies Magazine and Repository of Entertaining and Instructive Knowledge* (1792–3), the very first American women's magazine, was a novel venture in a volatile age. The American experiment in democracy, now a new and polyglot nation, had thrown many cultural rules and roles into question. Amidst this ideological flux, one prevailing orthodoxy was the idea that women were not expected to engage in the public sphere as speakers.[1] Yet dominant discourses proscribing women's self-representation faced various incursions by a democratizing culture: liberalizing standards for public speech were rousing and inflecting public debate, and the literary marketplace was also diversifying, offering up a widening array of narratives.[2] The more than 100 "ladies magazines" launched in America by 1830 partook of these conditions to subvert and redress the presumption of women's silence in the public realm.[3]

Early American women's magazines seemed tailor-made to promote the public responsiveness deemed largely improper for a lady. In the invitation to speak, and opportunity for debate and exchange, they promised women virtually revolutionary possibilities. But could they come through?

The first magazines wanted women's words, yet their very "democratic" openness threatened to limit women's presence in their pages, especially in the early years. The eighteenth-century convention of anonymous or pseudonymous publication may have shielded female contributors from postpublication ridicule and gendered accusations of un-"feminine" expression,[4] but it also made it easier for male writers to infiltrate women's magazine pages. In fact, several magazine scholars have argued that, as Patricia Okker put it, many of the earliest periodicals "were edited by men and consisted to a great extent of paternalistic advice for women."[5]

But the project of paternalism faltered in American women's magazines. Soon women contributors exploited available lapses and loopholes, finding ways to make their magazines sites for writing themselves out from under dominating male voices in the public domain.

ROBBING THE CRADLE OF LIBERTY:
THE CASE OF THE SILENCED SISTER

When paternalistic male authors spoke to women in the early magazines, they did so in three major modes: female impersonation, reader negation, or omission.

The very first magazine article in America to address the position of women was written by a man posing as a woman. On the eve of the Revolution, radical democrat Thomas Paine published his "Address on the Female Sex" in his *Pennsylvania Magazine* (1775–76). In the piece, the male writer literally takes women's part; he impersonates a female speaker—albeit to plead woman's case for speaking for herself.[6]

In the Early Republic, just as the first women's magazines were appearing, author Charles Brockden Brown picked up the same thread in a *Literary Magazine and American Register* (dates unavailable) series, "The Rights of Women." Brown similarly dramatizes women's silence while trying to end it. Writing in 1805, he captures the essence of the problem in Early Republican terms:

Pray, Madam, are you a Foederalist? She answers with the sarcasm of the unduly dispossessed: Surely, she replied, you are in jest. What! Ask a woman, shallow and inexperienced, as all women are known to be, especially with regard to these topics, her opinion on any political question! A list of her grievances follows: While I am conscious of being an intelligent moral being; while I see myself denied, in so many cases, the exercise of my own discretion, incapable of separate property; subject in all periods of my life to the will of another, on whose bounty I am made to depend for food and shelter; when I see myself, in my relation to society, regarded merely as a beast, as an insect, passed over, in the distribution of public duties, as absolutely nothing . . . it is impossible I should assent to their opinion, so long as I am conscious of moving and willing . . . No, I am no Foederalist.[7]

Brown's dialogue bespeaks the fact that, as Karen K. List has written, the early American press only indirectly discussed women as political actors, and early American magazines almost never did at all.[8] Brown's "Rights of Women" usefully makes that void visible. He articulates a complex of absences: *not* free, *not* represented, *no* Federalist, "absolutely nothing." The repeated negations that Brown writes into his female speaker's mouth evoke what she *is not*, and they underscore her absence by doing so secondhand. His dialogue thereby foregrounds the acute absence of a constructive language through which a woman speaker can positively represent where she stands, what she believes, and who she is, in public terms.

Unfortunately, the valuable efforts of men such as Paine and Brown, who wanted to expand women's public presence, are undercut somewhat by their formal reproduction of women's silence.[9] But what's more unfortunate is the fact that very few male writers in Early Republican magazines followed their lead in pushing for women's public expression.

Far more common than the likes of Paine or Brown are the ordinary men whose writing foreclosed possibilities for women's self-representation in public. One of the most common tactics they used was negation. A 1785 letter sequence published in the June, August, October, and November 1792, issues of the *Ladies' Magazine and Repository* exposes in detail some mechanics of this approach.

"Letters from a Brother to a Sister at a Boarding School" is a series of five letters, which seem both current and authentic when they appear in the magazine: they are printed in consecutive issues, and in letter format, including the salutations and original dates of writing. Yet the sequence, as published, tellingly distorts the definitive dynamic of the letter-writing process: the union of writer and reader through which a collaborative building of meaning takes place.[10] Only the brother's letters appear in the *Ladies' Magazine*. This one-sided presentation warps the basic equality of the correspondence relationship, concentrating the brother's voice while effacing the sister's response. Indeed, to readers of the magazine, her voice would seem doubly suppressed—by the male author of the letters, the brother, and by the male editor of the magazine, Gibbons.

The brother's August 1792 letter begins with "an extract from Dr. Richard Hey's dissertation" on "the strict though inexplicable connection between the body and the mind."[11] The brother, using Dr. Hey, instructs his sister that she should "regulate [the] course of life" because "the pleasures which have a tendency to dissipate and enervate, should be used with prudent reserve, lest they should introduce an habitual lassitude and depression, which may degenerate into melancholy." "Above all," proclaims the brother quoting Hey, "indulge your propensities of the benevolent kind."

It is not difficult to imagine why a brother might offer this lesson to his American sister. The excerpt conjoins two fundamental conceits of feminine gender obligations moving into the nineteenth century: women were to "regulate . . . pleasures" and "indulge benevolence." The excerpt nicely conflates an obviated form of self-interest (the avoidance of "lassitude and melancholy"), with "regulation," suggesting, among other things, that a woman's pursuit of happiness is linked with her virtuous self-restraint.

But when one more closely considers the source, a hidden, more threatening spin emerges. The male writer calls on the doctor's authority in what appears to be a constructive process aimed at modeling his sister's pursuit of a good life. He describes Hey's program as "such an excellent direction for the conduct of life, as is not easily to be equalled" [sic]. Yet Hey's "dissertation," we learn only later, is actually a treatise about suicide. It is not a book about living life, but about avoiding death—and by one's own hand. As such, the brother's ostensibly positive example of the sister's "direction in life" becomes, in fact, a negative anti-example, an admonition, a woeful warning.

The next letter, published in the October 1792 issue, continues to exude this ominous negativity. It begins with a backhanded compliment further attenuated by its faint praise: "Though your last letter is not free from errors," he points out, "accuracy is what I do not, at present, expect."[12] Even those minimal, implied expectations, however, are soon disturbed. He writes of the sister's "freedom and fertility of thought"—a phrase so resonant for women that it appears, affirmatively, in numerous contributions to the more self-assured and woman-authored women's magazines of the 1830s—here with the imputation of disease and catastrophe. "This letter," he initially commends, "abounds more with ideas than any former composition of yours that has come under my notice. This I consider a promising symptom." It is there that his rhetoric takes on an anxious edge. The brother continues in that vein, explaining, "your mind will [now] begin to exert its powers of invention, and to think for itself. This, then," he concludes, "is an important crisis."

The brother's negative reaction to his sister's expressive eloquence as a letter writer is particularly telling. Although a woman's letter-writing ability is a primary signal of her social competency, the sister's intellectual creativity and ability to think for herself is hardly seen by her brother as a sign of success. Instead, it is a "symptom." It is a signal of trouble or loss glimpsed, but not yet grasped. But it foretells a "crisis."

Can he stop it? The brother's mounting anxiety next condenses into anger, which seems only accentuated by Gibbons's placement of the fourth letter in the very next column of the *Ladies Magazine*'s October 1792 issue. The letter opens with naked chastisement. "The principle reason [for writing] is that I think it necessary to mention your faults," the brother dashes, and "whatever pain it may cost you," he continues, "I think myself obliged to say that, after such expectations as I had formed of you, I am greatly disappointed."[13] The brother's expectations of his sister may have everything to do with his expectations of himself. Are his designs foiled by her failure as a receiver of instructions, or his as the purveyor of them? Whose lapses lay behind his grievances?

The male writer moves to answer these questions—and at his female reader's expense. In the end, the brother resorts to denunciation, blaming the sister for an impudent or ignorant indifference to his absent (or omitted) instructions. "I kept in mind the directions I had given you," he thinks, "and was constantly cherishing the hope, that I could see them copied into your conduct; or at least that they would give some structure to your mind and influence in general your turn of character." In this curt letter of just two paragraphs, the writer's vexation is fully revealed: "I have been reviewing the rough copies of some of the letters which I sent you, and am still inclined to think, that, if you had at all imbibed the Spirit of them, you would have been a very different person from what you are."

Therein lies the rub. The male writer had intended to implement a "structure" for his female reader's "character" and, in fact, apparently believed that, with some assistance from an acknowledged male expert, he was carrying out this mission. But what's missing, at least for readers of the *Ladies Magazine*, are the specific details. The brother's letters, as published, lack the authorized and effective discourse necessary to bring his designs to fruition. If only the reading sister had somehow imbibed the "Spirit" of his intentions, she would be different from "what"—not who—she is.

The brother's closing "intention," one of alarm, is "to rouse in you, even now, though it be at the eleventh hour, a desire to make the best of the opportunities that still remain." Despite the apparent exigency of the situation, once again the male writer again chooses tacit negatives, an "instructive" strategy already pretested to fail. The letter concludes with a series of rhetorical questions. Evinced is what the sister has *not* done: fulfill her brother's unspoken expectations; obey his incomplete instructions; and somehow render herself independent (of him) despite denial of the most proper means of doing so.

Even though the brother has enjoyed the presentational privilege provided by the male editor, Gibbons, he still suffers from a much larger lack of structural support. He does not have the established, patriarchal authority he needs to warrant his mandate.[14] Owing to this deficiency, the fifth and final letter in the November issue recommends the reading of two male-authored manuals, both written on the subject of the "proper government of children." Are such books for her, or for her as-yet-unconceived offspring? Befuddled by his position, the negating brother finally puts all on a blind demand for obedience.

The third kind of male speaker is more well meaning than the brother, but just as incapable of rightly representing the American sister. He uses a language of omission. A narrator, this speaker propounds the many truncated parables of miserable and fallen females that appear in the early magazines. Foregrounding female suffering, these numerous contributions encapsulate female experience as the inexorable onset of dire distress.

Since written by amateur authors, these pieces do not fully conform to literary expectations for the period. They could reflect Nancy K. Miller's characterization of eighteenth-century fiction as narratives of the heroine's "one misstep";[15] yet that one false move is rarely revealed. Those that do reveal the mistake generally make clear that the heroine's suffering arose through no fault of her own. These narratives could represent the seeds of the sentimental, soon to become a marked "feminine" mode. Some are mere one-paragraph deathbed scenes, which Ann Douglas argues is a definitive element of the sentimental mode.[16] Still, it is typically mothers or young women who do the dying, not the innocent young children who center Douglas's analysis.[17] And few of the narratives glimpse the broader ideological aims of the sentimental story. At most, they offer a curtailed explanation of the process by which miserable women "fall."[18] Almost none offer a real spiritual rationale for the heroine's trials.[19]

Take, for example, "The Beggar Girl," a three-paragraph piece published in Samuel White's New York journal, the *Weekly Visitor, or Ladies' Miscellany* (1802–12), in November 1803. "Have pity on a wretched orphan," it opens, with the girl's "tears trickling down her care-worn cheeks, and her bosom heaving with sighs, that seemed to rend the heart from whence they came."[20] The abject figure approaches a "beautiful young creature" on the street, as the writer "draw[s] nearer for the purpose of hearing their discourse."

No names are given to this most abstract of entities. The poor girl then reveals that her father died, and that her mother, "afflict[ed] by the dreadful news," "like a drooping lily . . . withered and died," with her daughter clasped in her arms. Immediately, "our little all was seized by merciless creditors," she continues, "and friendless and unprotected, I'm doomed to wander, and prey to misery and fatigue." The woman passerby then murmurs, "God bless you, in such a tender, melancholy, impressive tone . . ."

that "borne on every breeze," it seemed telegraphed through town. The male narrator admits that he cannot find the words to finish the story: "'tis impossible to describe how affected I was," he submits. So he ends it there, assuring readers vaguely that the beggar girl "is now in a place, secure from every evil."

Another example is "A Fragment," published in the *Visitor* the previous February 12, 1803. The two-paragraph piece opens: "Whence that downcast look . . . those tears . . . and why those heart-rending sighs? Tell me fair maid the sorrows that rend thy bosom . . . ," he bids.[21] The maiden can only "rais[e] her eyes" and "with a look that conveyed to my breast an idea of persecuted innocence." She speaks only elliptical phrases, her speech seemingly broken up by sobs as well as narrative lapses. She breathes: "slander, that destroyer of peace . . . ," then continues, tangentially, that "I have waited in vain . . . no one on whom to rely for protection . . . no one to plead an orphan's case . . . I sink under the weight of unmerited obloquy." To these direful phrases, the writer cannot respond. Instead, he moves to end the piece. In a final paragraph of only two sentences, he turns away, muttering a series of abstract questions to the heavens or the air, but not to the maiden.

"Sarah—A Fragment," published in the *Visitor* the year before (December 31, 1802), is similarly the plaint of an orphan which, in its three-quarters of a column, can hardly explain why its pathetic subject appears "with tears streaming down her cheeks," crying out, "Can I hope that Heaven will hear my complaint, when a father turns his ear from it? Can I hope that charity will relieve a child whom its mother has also forsaken?"[22]

These estranged women speak in public only in desperation, and get heard only because they are overheard by male narrators. They thereby evoke the dimensions of women's limited speech in the public domain. Controlled by sentimentality, encased in their own vulnerability, women speak publicly only when they must, in pleading for help. The male narrators who give them limited representation neither elaborate their stories nor substantively assist them through a plot. Instead, the contributions either end with vague implications of some resolution, or simply cease when the male narrator, as if stymied by the scene and situation, drops the enterprise.

These examples reveal what early women writers were up against at the outset. The negating brother of the brother-sister letters was in fact a common Early Republican literary figure. In the allegedly more egalitarian frame of American democracy, the paternalist power the brother wants is difficult to justify—especially so soon. Although British magazines for women expertly mingled "compliment and chastisement in the service of didactic intent,"[23] many early American articles bungle the attempt, failing to find the words and ways to serve didactic aims. In the highly-promoted democratic context of the magazine in America, male writers found themselves consistently thwarted by an absence of rhetorical and logical means to claim the patriarchal authority they wanted. Thus, numerous frustrated, forbidding brothers appeared, young men whose lateral relationships to their American sisters still did not neutralize expectations of hierarchical authority over them.[24] Even if they couldn't handle it.

To complicate matters more, the apparent collaboration of the male editor, Gibbons, actually both underlined and undermined the brother's aims. As Cathy Davidson has discussed, early American printers such as Gibbons shaped textual meanings mainly through their use of type treatments and excisions or additions to texts.[25] Gibbons overtly displayed this editorial power when he offered an extended excerpt of Wollstonecraft's *The Rights of Woman* in the August 1792 issue—the same issue in which the brother introduces his sister to Dr. Hey. Gibbons presented the excerpt as an interview, putting questions to Wollstonecraft, then briefly quoting from the book as her answer. Although his direct quotations help, the male editor still appears to be imposing his patriarchal power over the woman speaker, since he controls both questions and answers.

Yet Gibbons had different interests at heart, interests that shift the balance of power. The Wollstonecraft excerpt is actually an advertisement, a "teaser," for copies of *The Rights of Woman*, which the printer had available for sale in his North Third Street bookshop in Philadelphia.[26] His marketplace interests trump patriarchal ones since Gibbons uses his editorial power less to dominate the woman writer than to entice women readers to buy and read the book for themselves.

Similarly, the one-sided presentation of the male voice in the brother-sister letter sequence might appear to foreclose female response. Yet the marked absence of the sister may actually have encouraged readers to want more, perhaps to enter the dialogue and answer the figure of the negating brother themselves. When the democratic dress of the women's magazine is seen surrounding the expectations of collaborative interaction shared by both the letter and the interview format, the sister's silencing could be seen to function much as the Wollstonecraft Q & A did: as an enticement or provocation to go further, as an advertisement for reader response. Certainly that reader participation within the magazine was as pivotal to Gibbons's long-term financial success as book sales out of his shop were.

The many narratives of omission also tended to incite redress of women's silence. In virtually all of these narratives, the central women characters are orphans, at times specifically said to be disadvantaged by the absence of the maternal care thought crucial to the rearing of young ladies of the day. Paternalist male authors demonstrate clearly in their narratives that they are incapable of filling the gap; as narrators and authors they are absent fathers or, at best, inadequate fathers to the suffering female figures.

But women readers were encouraged by the magazine form, its marketing, and often by the content of these narratives themselves to become the surrogate mothers, the sisters, aunts, and friends that voiceless women needed to find their way. "The Beggar Girl" is but one example among many that somehow show that woman's negated and needy condition rightfully elicits constructive response from women "everywhere."

To write themselves out from under these mechanisms of male silencing, early Republican readers and writers exploited the narrative opportunities, multiple and novel contexts, and collective practices made available by early women's magazines. Taken together, their contributions began to develop ways to press the feminine case for the self-representation promised by American democracy and the American magazine at their birth.

WRITING WOMEN IN: THE WOMAN'S ANGLE

Since women writers faced the problem of becoming visible, of overcoming absence, they worked quite directly from the masculine practices of authority and authorship that were more easily seen. Contributors took on narratives of omission, for example, by filling in some gaps in the story so as to demonstrate that the framework men wrote for women didn't hold up or yield a happy ending for anybody. Others attacked strategies of negation by turning the tables on male attitudes and prerogatives, revealing the previously hidden—and widely undesirable—effects of unjust authority.

In general, contributions did not take up radical subjects. They tended to stick to conventionally gendered questions, but to pursue them onto uncommon ground. The early magazines are filled with submissions on matrimony and its meanings; seduction and its consequences; and virtue, rightly defined. But in the treatment of these topics, contributors often reveal previously invisible implications. For example, matrimonial essays invariably raise embedded questions about what have lately been dubbed "the rules."[27] That is, they take up the unwritten rules of female obedience, subservience, and dependence in marriage.

Very often, matrimonial essays in early magazines become meditations on the failure of marriage to conform to its own rules, to live up to its promises. The author of the 1792 contribution to the *Ladies Magazine and Repository*, "Thoughts on Old Maids," for example, questions the uninformed cultural reading of unmarried women that has been carried over from the Old World into the new one unchanged. "Custom has annexed to an Old Maid singularity—ill-nature, prudery, and several other disagreeable impressions, which are a great injustice," the author believes.[28] Many unmarried women "act very prudently in declining entering into matrimony with such suitors as they often have," she contends.

This contributor is probably intimately familiar with the gendered injunction—and cultural necessity—of a woman's careful choice of a husband. The growing range of novels and stories that trace the consequences of imprudent alliances, running the political gamut from Susanna Rowson's best-selling sentimental story *Charlotte Temple* (1794 in the United States) to Wollstonecraft's *Maria, or the Wrongs of Woman* (1794), ensures familiarity with this one, all-too-important women's plotline. But the contributor brings an ordinary woman's vision to the story. She arrives at neither dramatic self-destruction (offered by Rowson) nor political diatribe (given by Wollstonecraft), but instead focuses on the everyday, unfair double bind good women can face: those who proceed with the necessary care may find that their virtue and values force them to forgo matrimony. It is wrong, the contributor concludes, that such unmarried women should suffer for their very fidelity to the gendered grammar of the marriage plot.

These issues, marriage and spinsterhood, typify even larger meditations on the many unwritten rules controlling women's stories of all sorts. The "old maid" is a preoccupation among contributors throughout the nineteenth century because this figure raises the prospect of a major contradiction in early-nineteenth-century terms: the lady as autonomous individual.

"Thoughts on Old Maids" was the first piece in American women's magazine history to talk about the unheard-of possibility that a woman might live respectably on her own—but it would not be the last. This first example, in fact, lays the groundwork for many subsequent treatments. To approach the markedly alternative lifestyle of feminine autonomy, the contributor moves carefully but cleverly, affirming that female autonomy can be the proper outcome of faithful adherence to authorized gender rules. Thus, without abolishing the prevailing gender discourse, the contributor nevertheless moves to alter it. And the logical and rhetorical strategy she uses—of following on all the emergent rules of feminine conduct until they collide in moral contradiction—will become an increasingly common tactic in women's politics and magazine writing through the antebellum period, culminating in its frequent use within the first-generation feminist magazines of the 1850s.

Such double binds and double standards are prevalent themes in early American women's magazine writing. A January 1807 letter "To the Editor" of White's *Weekly Visitor, or Ladies' Miscellany* takes up the injustice of marital inequality. "There is something capriciously cruel in what most men expect from their wives," the writer observes.[29] Reproving, with due propriety of course, the gendered double standard as an emotional injustice that culture has ratified, the writer explains that husbands "are displeased with [their wives] for seeming to feel any jealousy of their fidelity, even if they know they deserve it."

What's worse, she continues, authorized gender relations prohibit a woman from contesting unfair marriage practices, even if she were to do so with a "feminine" eye toward sustaining marriage concord. "A man dislikes that his wife should express any symptoms of discontent," she notes, "when he declares his intention to leave her and dine at a tavern with his friends." "Yet," she projects, "he would not be pleased to hear her say, especially if he thought she spoke her thoughts, 'Pray, my dear, go: I shall be just as happy without you.'"

To make her position visible, the contributor has used role reversal, a simple narrative shift that sustained much of women's magazine writing over time. This contributor does not suggest that a husband's freedom to live and act as he chooses ought to be equally shared by wives—but some women did in later nineteenth-century women's magazines, especially the more progressive publications produced in the cities of the Northeast. Neither does she explicitly propose that a husband's commitment to marriage ought to curtail his freedoms in leisure time, centralizing his wife, home, and family, as other women writers argued ardently beginning about 1830. Even so, the logical pivot for each of these parallel lines of nineteenth-century gender discourse can be read here. By exposing that a husband probably would not appreciate the treatment he routinely proffers to his wife, this writer subtly proposes a more egalitarian understanding of the cultural rights and responsibilities of women and men. Turning the tables on the masculine prerogative to remain autonomous after marriage—a move it takes a woman writer to make—the vast web of double standards applied to men's and women's conduct, here in both public life and private relationships, is opened up for discussion.

The many early contributions like these take logical and rhetorical steps to bring to light the perspectives and experiences of women, the previously hidden, omitted or suppressed *effects* of attitudes and practices accepted by a culture constructive of masculine privilege. The earliest women's magazines are full of submissions that similarly reveal everyday expressions of gender inequality or devaluation, many through women's application of the simple folk wisdom that "what's good for the gander is good for the goose." Such examples as the *Weekly Visitor's* "Vindication of the Tongues of Women,"[30] many essays, like the one in New York's *Lady's Weekly Miscellany* (1805–08) concerning "The Mental Endowments of Women,"[31] numerous salutes to "Female Heroism,"[32] and articles variously asserting "The Respect Due to Females,"[33] work similarly, applying basic reversals or situating women's experiences within "masculine" settings in order to question the operations of gender hierarchy in everyday life. Presented in the "democratic" context of the early American women's magazine, these various contributions raise and represent discontinuities between democratic promises and women's position in Early Republican culture.

A related strategy in early women's magazine writing is the imaginative use of new—and male-coded—contexts made permissible by the magazine's polygeneric form and public identity. In the July 1792 issue of the *Ladies Magazine and Repository*, for example, the female author of "On Matrimonial Obedience" appropriates the space she needs to interrogate patriarchal law from the inside. The contributor begins on confirmed ground, with an accredited claim of feminine propriety: "the word *obey*, in the promise or vow to be made by the *woman* [is] very improper," she writes, "and ought not to be."[34] But when she next explains why, she begins to move to a new place. "Obliging a woman to make a *vow to obey* their husbands [is] . . . obliging them to perjure themselves," she writes. By mingling the "feminine" language of decorum with the "masculine" discourse of courtroom conduct, she brings two sets of gendered values together.

Newly situated somewhere beyond the feminine realm, the writer uses an explosive analogy to push her experience further into the public sphere. "I object to the word *obey* . . . for where I have sworn, or even promised to obey any man, I must on honour consider myself as having sworn or promised to obey him in all things, at all times. In a word, I have bound myself to be his *slave*, until he is pleased to release me, which in the matrimonial world, is an occurrence that I believe seldom happens." The contributor's comparison makes slavery a kind of "anti-touchstone," a means to better position her claim to higher—that is, to equal—authority within gender hierarchy. She does not attempt to condemn slavery; indeed, her self-serving use of the institution to delineate her own wrongful place on the social scale might even serve to help legitimize it.[35]

Nevertheless, the point has been to create a politicized space within which to press the feminine case. The contributor does pivot from her slavery reference directly into an imaginary courtroom, which possibly suggests that the "peculiar institution," just like the marital one, calls for cross-examination. In any case, the contributor now becomes an attorney in the midst of a trial, asking, "Why, therefore, is the word *obey* still preserved in our service, when it would be easy to leave it out; and when, in fact, we know that it is virtually left out by nine out of ten who enter into that holy state?" Tellingly, the one-sided obligation is undemocratic in a simple sense: the vast majority of marriages, she testifies, already begin on this rhetorically equal plane, and to her mind, majority rules.

The scales of justice need adjustment. So, like an attorney, the writer demands that evidence be brought forward to support the continuation of the wrongful practice being tried: "You may say, perhaps, that the word *obey* as it appears in our service, means only that the wife is to obey in all things lawful—Yes—But can you prove that *obey* will admit of this restrictive interpretation?—Can you also prove," she insists, "that husbands in general, will admit of the very favourable construction you are pleased to put upon it?" Her conclusion to this cross-examination is brief, but decisive: "I am afraid not."

The writer is now in a rhetorical position to offer a brief but broad-reaching summation. She proposes a reconfiguration that ripples with ramifications: the roles of leader and led ought to be gender neutral, and premised on merit, talent, and experience, rather than received convention or unreasonable law. "Suppose we leave out of our consideration the many women of superior judgment, of our acquaintance," she grants, "it will still be allowed that . . . there is no woman whose understanding is so very barren, but that she may at sometimes take the lead in command with a better effect than her husband." Appropriating public standards for private relations, the writer advances toward an egalitarian model of the marriage relationship in which the wife is neither slave nor subordinate. At least by rhetorical formulation, wife and husband are hereby created equal.

It is a reflection of widespread public elaboration of American democracy then occurring in the press that the contributor is tagged "A Matrimonial Republican." But the pseudonym also suits her for other reasons.

Her appropriation of a masculine public space, and deployment of the legalistic language that space demands, has opened an important door. Bringing private relations to court, the Matrimonial Republican begins to formulate a critical ideological bridge across which later women writers (and others) would march: rhetorically at least, she bridges the gap between the public and the private domains, perhaps the foundational dichotomy from which wrongful gender configurations have historically ensued.

LETTER AND ADDRESS: GENDERED GENRES AND THEIR USES

The simple reasoning of role reversal—that turnabout is fair play—quickly becomes a standard practice in early women's magazines, informing authorial voices as well as expository practices. When used within certain contexts, such reversals can ramify well beyond the page and into the social world.

In several instances very early on, authorial role reversals occur within the epistolary form. In two ways, this is not surprising. First of all, more generally, the letter is a natural fit for the early magazines. In fact, its formal characteristics overlap those of the magazine itself: both act as a nexus for ongoing exchange controlled by collaborating reader-writers. Little wonder then that letters "To the Editor" and missives to and among readers populate even the earliest colonial magazines, and that letters remain an earmark of American women's magazines to the present time.

But letters have long carried and conveyed particularly resonant meanings for women. Historically, as numerous scholars have discussed, the letter is a gendered genre, carrying special meanings, privileges, and limitations to women and men writers respectively.[36] Although cultural prescriptions about letter-writing decorum were shifting by the eighteenth century, generally with the result of degrading women's epistolarity as strictly private, nonliterary, and emotional,[37] the letter remained a valuable form for women. Cultural prescriptions inveighed against women's engagements with novels, romances, political essays, and classical works—but never letters. The letter was perhaps the one form of self-expression and exchange that had always been available to women writers and readers, and was widely accredited for their use.[38] That's yet another reason why the sister's silence in the brother-sister letters may have incited reader response.

Although both Early Republican men and women had access to letter writing, only women gained a special access and status under its auspices.

The presumed "natural" affiliation of women and letter writing is affirmed and reinforced in early American women's magazines from the very start of the tradition. Gibbons's *Ladies Magazine and Repository* headlines the publication of reader letters as "Select Letters or Specimens of Female Literature" in its earliest issues.[39] Early women's magazines at times printed letters under the editorial heading "models of female comportment." Over time, epistolary conventions became a kind of shorthand for articles, essays, and other generic contributions addressed to and written by women. As the periodical for women gained shape through 1830, various types of contributions written about culturally constituted "women's issues," subjects such as virtue, marriage, motherhood, and "female character," were often collected across various editions in columns editorially earmarked "Letters on . . ." these themes.

The socially sanctioned, gender-accredited form of the letter helped many early women's magazine contributors claim a remarkable degree of authorial agency. A letter from "A Young Lady to Her Seducer," published in White's *Weekly Visitor* of April 4, 1807, uses the letter to accomplish a crucial authorial turn for women, and one which, through both the letter and the magazine, carries implications as important for women writers and readers as for the Lady herself.

The issue of seduction had been a major story in the *Visitor* prior to the publication of the young lady's letter. A lead story opening the January 8, 1803, edition, *Seduction: A Tale Founded upon Fact*, reads like a late-eighteenth-century didactic novel, part story, part authorial intervention aimed at controlling reader behavior. A poem, "The Seducer," had appeared the issue before, and had envisioned in verse the voice of recreant men. The April 30, 1803, issue carried an article outlining the negative "Effects of Seduction." "Seduction," a definitive piece of admonishment even if it was only a fragment, appeared less than a year later (March 31, 1804). On June 9, 1804, "Seduction" appeared. "Thoughts on Seduction," an explanation of the problem in social terms, came out in the October 27, 1804, issue. "The Fatal Effects of Seduction: A Tale" opened a spring issue of the journal, running between May 11 and June 1, 1805. Each of these contributions, all published anonymously except one that carried a pseudonym, approached seduction for a similar purpose: warning about its consequences. Nevertheless, each added new shades of meaning to the discussion. Some contributions dealing with the effects of seduction—one an essay, the other a "tale"—may have been written by women.

These submissions all share a tone of admonition and a sense of narrative remove; all warn women by edict to avoid faithless seducers. Although all of these previously published *Visitor* pieces are suggestive of one element or other of The Lady's letter, none combined female authorship with a woman's story the way her letter did. None of these earlier articles spoke with the authority of experience, or proceeded to name names. None of them turned the tables on male misconduct, revealing while also reviling its previously unseen effects. The previous publication of contributions on the subject of seduction may have created a supportive environment for The Lady to publicize her seduction. But the "Letter from a Young Lady to Her Seducer" represents the culmination of that tradition. Like the letter format in which it is written, the contribution inherited the past, and moved beyond it.

The young lady begins confidently, using the intimacy of the letter strategically, to pave the way for a heart-to-heart confrontation where, arguably, she would have the upper hand. "I write not to justify myself to yo[u]; you deserve not—" she begins, "but while I lay open my heart, I desire you would examine *your own*—."[40] Using the audience dynamics of the letter (and the magazine) to her advantage, the young lady questions the addressee both pointedly and declaratively: "What must your sensations be when you recollect that you have violated all laws, divine and human; broken through every principle of virtue, and every tie of humanity; that you have offered an insult to the kind genius of hospitality, the benevolent spirit of good-neighborhood, and the sacred powers of friendship."

The rhetorical structure and rhythm of this opening paragraph, which initially emphasizes evocative dualities—"divine" and "human," "principles" and "ties"—soon foregrounds a woman's cultural perspective of the codes her lover had breached. The "principles" at issue are not those of democracy, but of "virtue." He has scorned a gendered complex of values that women are meant to hold dear: "hospitality," "benevolence," and "the sacred powers of friendship."

She is confident enough in the form to press her case further, and to get angry. She assaults the "masculine" characteristics and cultural privileges her seducer has exploited: "Was it not sufficient that you added my name to the list of your infamous triumphs? . . . that you had ranked me among the daughters of wretchedness and ignomy?" [sic] she asks. But that's not all; she continues in progressive phrases: "Deprived me of my father, my all of comfort, and my all of hope? Were not these things sufficient," she asserts, implying the excess of his prerogative, the extremity of his wrongs, "without adding to them the baseness of publicly speaking of me in the streets, in language that a gentleman would not have used to the vilest wanton that ever breathed."

The writer's list of grievances bespeaks the absolute loss of her identity—personal, familial, and cultural—at the hands of an ignoble man whose "triumph" is to "deprive" her of even those accredited qualities of selfhood allowed and allotted to women. What is worse, he has violated her in public. Exposed as an estranged woman, she could be utterly undone. Yet she turns her loss to consolation, her isolation to a kind of triumphant embrace: "Weak, unhappy man! I am not ashamed of defeat," she declares.

In this letter, righteous anger about male mistreatment sets up a reversal that represents at least a rhetorical victory for the woman's identity and point of view. The seducer may have "ruined" his abandoned mistress to the public mind, but in the context of the woman's letter, his ignoble deceit, base language, and inhuman rending of culturally ratified rules of interpersonal conduct have *ruined him*. The story of seduction and abandonment is rewritten here. The seducer, rather than the person seduced, is seen to be weak, miserable, debased, and defeated. He, not she, is destroyed. Denouncing her presumed conqueror as perverse and monstrous, the writer fully unmans him.

It is a triumph of the woman's perspective that touches reality on so many points that it glimpses a whole new world, and one where women's ways prevail. Once shared with women readers, the rhetorical strategies of this victory had enormous ramifications for women's narratives both in magazines and outside them in the decades to come. For, as one feminist critic has written, "the endeavor to enter and re-interpret cultural prescriptions from previously hidden directions, the sense of power derived from perceiving oneself as central, as subject" is pivotal to personal as well as cultural empowerment.[41]

After all, though abandoned, this Lady is hardly alone. The magazine is a place for her to expose her male seducer before a public—to do unto him, through the magazine, what he has done unto her in the streets. Unmaking him in this place, she also publicly constitutes herself. This self-making is marked by the attachment of her Christian name, "Eliza," to the published letter.

Furthermore, Eliza's act of self-creation is multiply inviting of readers' emulation. Her letter speaks to the implied audience of the *Visitor* as much as to its addressee. These magazine readers are doubly engaged: by the dynamic expectations of the epistolary form and the reader-responsive climate of the magazine. Such overlapping invitations to reader involvement in Eliza's story push for audience ratification and reiteration of similar acts of world-changing self-representation by women.

AUDIENCE ENGAGEMENTS: COLLABORATION AND THE COLLECTIVE AUTHORIZATION OF GENDER DISCOURSE

The epistolary relations at play in Eliza's contribution are suggestive of the numerous forms of audience engagement encouraged by the magazine's own brand of female reader. A November 1802 contribution to White's *Weekly Visitor*, "The Criterion of Virtue," explicitly incorporates that audience participation as both a figure for and a means to pursue rhetorical and cultural goals. The writer, "V.," raises with readers the language of politics and the politics of language. She envisions reader collaboration in her effort to redefine the popular understanding of "feminine virtue," a pivotal gendered term that was repeatedly deployed to advance women toward more public roles.

"It is, I believe, extremely common, in the appropriation of words to ideas, to give them erroneous significations, or attribute greater latitude to general terms than they were originally intended to express," V. begins.[42] Since her sights are set on the reform of a pervasive popular belief, she finds that the magazine is her only place to turn: "I have often, though vainly, wished to see the criterion of virtue, as it respects our sex, properly established," so "it shall be the employment of a serious hour to assign, with as much precision as my slender knowledge will admit, the distinct and proper claims of the highest grace a woman can possess."

Although officially attenuated by the writer's admission of "slender knowledge" (a frequent female disclaimer in women's magazines through the nineteenth century), the ensuing article pursues a larger understanding of a powerfully packed concept. Since she is seeking group consensus, this writer takes pains to image explicitly the collective space more generally figured by the women's magazine. For her, the most suitable workspace is not the contentious courtroom of the Matrimonial Republican, but the more congenial conversation place of the drawing room. At home in the magazine, she imagines herself surrounded by female company and asks just "a moment's indulgence" before she proceeds.

With her audience now arrayed, the writer-speaker moves to the task before them all. "Virtue, if I understand its implications rightly," she leads, "is a combination not a solitary grace, when meant to include female excellence." Continuing, she complicates the oversimplifying metonymy of chastity-as-virtue: "Chastity, (although the fairest ornament our sex can boast, and without which no woman can be estimable) is yet but a *single* virtue" and so it hardly captures the "whole of female excellence."

Pointing to complexities of the term in experience and practice, she argues "it is as possible for a woman to be chaste without being good, as for a man to be industrious without being honest." The gendered analogy she uses, wherein women's chastity should be but one indication of her goodness, and men's industriousness but one of his honesty, helps raise complications in gender categories. The use of the culturally visible disjunction between male industry and honesty corroborates the previously unseen inadequacy of the equation between female chastity and virtue.

"Virtue is an aggregate," V. asserts. Her "new and improved" virtue requires an expanded assessment of women's "estimable" qualities, beginning with chastity, but also including such qualities as intelligence, benevolence, and moral strength. As V. derives the necessary components of a new virtue through analysis of its cultural contradictions and inadequacies, she simultaneously breaks it down and builds it up. The process implicates the current understanding of the term as faulty, while also raising it to an elevated standard more difficult to achieve. Does raising standards promote higher attainment and status, or prevent it?

The answer depends upon the cultural conditions of reception. Judging from the dominant middle-class gender ideal of the antebellum era, V.'s version of female excellence was on the right track. In her own time, what V.'s letter captures is the expectation of reception, facilitated by the early women's magazine, that helped make such visions later come to life. The project of the contribution, to revise and ratify gender discourse, images as it calls upon the *Visitor's* potential to mobilize its middle-class female audience.

V.'s letter therefore divulges a critical function of the early women's magazine that was variously utilized by American women. Turning on the "erroneous signification" attached to the powerfully gendered notion of woman's virtue, the contribution demonstrates that cultural reconfigurations of gender discourse are rightful and necessary—and require women's active and collective effort. Woman writer and women readers work together, through the magazine, to raise, revise, and authorize new or missing meanings for gendered terms. At the same time, the magazine disseminates both those meanings and the participatory methods by which they are achieved. V.'s piece not only demonstrates women's participation in the development of gender discourse; also, its visibility in the democratic magazine seems to endorse collaboration and consensus as the rightful means of ratifying the cultural codes by which American women would consent to live.

COLLECTIVE ENGAGEMENTS: AUDIENCE
EXPECTATIONS AND NARRATIVE RE-VISIONS

As women's magazines began to proliferate in early America, contributions show an increasing awareness of such engaged and able audiences. Submissions apparently written by women, for other women, respond with increasing sophistication and strength to male silencing. Increasingly, they dare to frankly reveal injustices visited upon the female sex through the application and policing of conventional gender rules, and to portray women's righteous responses as justified by the very spirit of those laws.

A "New Trait in the Female Character," an 1801 narrative published in the *Lady's Magazine and Musical Repository* (1801–2), vividly describes a woman's principled rebellion against—and triumph over—what else? the patriarchal marriage plot. The contribution relays the story of a good woman consigned by her father to a marriage not of her choice Mr. F—a man not her match in "brilliancy" or talent. Indeed, we are told at the top, Mr. F's "sole merit consisted in the possession of great wealth; a kind of merit which seldom interests the young, but to which parents usually attach a very high value."[43]

At first, the daughter directly confronts her powerlessness and dehumanization in a marriage market where she is bought and sold for the interests of everyone but herself. She expresses her belief "that, with respect to marriage, she could not separate her interests from her taste, that, in such a state, the first of all requisites were mutual affection." Moreover, she continues, no parent "should have made [such a] promise without consulting her." Alas, to no avail. The parties to the bargain would not "be defeated in their purpose"; trying to break her down or beat her into submission, they "loaded her with reproaches and invectives whenever they were alone with her." "The anger of the father was even carried so far," the writer dares to report, "as to throw a knife at her, which wounded her in the face." Yet no matter what punishments she received—which included being deprived of her solace in books, and in playing her harpsichord—"she would not allow the wound to be cured."

Still holding onto her outrage, the woman one day "tranquilly reported, that she consented to marry Mr. F—." What she had actually done is plot her cleverly gendered revenge, a plan revealed to readers. Using the very qualities and "feminine" position that had entrapped her in a loveless marriage not of her choice, she devised an escape. "Her husband was soon subjugated by the influence of her mental superiority and attractions: She became sovereign mistress of the house, and of all the wealth he possessed; she gradually made use of this power.—Her expenditure was immense—

her benevolence unbounded," we're told. "In a few years her husband was worth nothing—all his property had vanished."

"Your money," said his wife finally, "was the cause of my misery: now, thank God! Not a farthing remains." "I have now ruined you, but I will not forsake you," she continues. "You would starve, for you can do nothing for yourself," she jibes. "I will take care of you: but for this time I will have my own conditions."

These conditions reflect the gist of the magazine contribution itself: the virtuous woman demands that she live out her life on her own terms. Since also freed of subjection to her father, who "died the interval," she establishes a business in the millinery trade, and makes a home with her sister. And "she lodged her husband in a small apartment, at a considerable distance from her own residence, and pays him an annuity on the express condition that he shall never come near her."

It is difficult to know if the "new trait" at issue in this contribution is the woman's independence or her attainment of just desserts. But in either case, the fantasy here is that a good woman can use the very stipulations of "feminine" gender identity to find some form of justice. Still, the content of the contribution is multiply mediated; it is a letter extract that relays thirdhand the reportedly true story of an unnamed woman. The writer's responsibility for both authorship and expressed content is obfuscated. In a short time, however, such masks and evasions faded from the pages of women's magazines as contributions grew more confident in their audiences and in strategies of constructive critique and revolt.

The desire—the demand—for voice grows increasingly apparent in women's magazines moving into the nineteenth century. By the 1820s, contributors begin writing quite sophisticated tales of independent women, and they confidently rely on engaged audiences to collaborate in giving them full meaning and impact. A striking example of these critical developments is an April 1828 story published by Sarah Hale in her (American) Ladies' Magazine (1828–36). The story rereads as it rewrites the tale of an autonomous woman, or "old maid," named Margery Bethel.

The story begins with a biographical sketch notable for the scantness of the evidence it supplies. "Margery Bethel was an inhabitant of Danvers, Mass. It is not certain that she was a native of that town, nor is the year of her birth accurately known; but in 1719, she bore such evident marks of age, that she became distinguished by the appellation peculiar to unmarried females . . .—she was called an old maid."[44] Margery's story would have been a romance narrative were it not for the dereliction of the male partner. She "had been a famous beauty,—her several admirers, and, it was conjectured, was once engaged to be married. But her lover, as lovers have often done since the example of Phaon, proved a recreant."

With this ruination of the "feminine" romance plot, Margery is on her own. She becomes an early prototype of the emergent sentimental-domestic heroine, the female focal point of the ascending literary genre that demonstrated a woman's achievement of self-reliance through the repeated exercise of her virtuous character.[45] "The disconsolate fair-one . . . neither rhymed nor raved, nor made any attempt to drown herself. She acted a much more common, and, indeed, more feminine part. She became sad, think [sic], and taciturn; and finally, as her beauty waned, she seemed to resign herself uncomplainingly, to neglect and celibacy. . . . She grew old, and she faded, as every fair girl will do . . . and was called ugly." The writer's structure and tone here suggest her awareness of and confidence in her reading audience. She can condense whole volumes of Bethel's history in a single detached and slightly sarcastic sentence because she knows women readers will have heard this story before, and will fill in the gaps for themselves.

As if this seemingly inexorable fate were not punishing enough to the mistreated Margery, the writer then interjects a pointed parallel to the social conditions constraining actual women living in the nonfiction world: "[T]here is another evil to which women are subjected," she asserts. "It is to have cultivated minds, and yet be confined to a society that does not understand and cannot appreciate their talents and intelligence. This frequently occurs." And so Margery Bethel's story becomes an allegory of the effects of woman's silence, of her absence from public mind.

The mystery of Margery's temperament slowly deepens into a larger communal distrust. Since Margery lived alone, and "never received company, no one knew much about her management. But the less they knew, the more they guessed; till finally, as she grew older and more reserved, they first called her odd—then cross—then strange—and then a witch!"

"The case of Margery made a great bustle," drawing scrutiny from the highest authorities in the town. Their first response is to hurl negations, in an effort to suppress the powers they imagine her to possess: "Her supposed compact with the spirit of the devil was regretted, or condemned, sighed over, or inveighed against," until these measures proved insufficient. Finally, it was "the opinion of all that something had to be done."

Not surprisingly, "the minister, the two deacons, and two of the most influential and pious men belonging to the church, were chosen to visit her, at her dwelling, and propound certain questions; and, from her answers, it was concluded, the full proof of her guilt, which no one doubted, would be obtained." The writer's elevated sarcasm conveys her contempt for this bogus interplay, in which male authorities blot out the possibility of a woman's self-expression by writing answers to their own questions before they are even asked of the subject—and at her expense. Poor Margery "was totally ignorant of the honor intended her," the writer wryly remarks, "as it had been judged expedient to take her by surprise as the most likely method of eliciting truth from one whose study was to deceive."

Fearful and uncomprehending of Margery's story, the male leadership of Danvers becomes enmeshed in a tense mystery plot. "The gentlemen . . . silently drew near the door," led by the minister who "heard a sound within. He paused, then motioned the party to advance, and they all cautiously crept forward, and all distinctly heard the same noise." The men could not decipher it, but all agreed on what it was not: "It was not like mortal conversation; it was a low, but continued, and monotonous sound, such as none of them ever recollected before to have heard. They all trembled."

As they eavesdrop on Margery, they recognize only that she seems to be speaking a language alien and unfamiliar to them. Since they lack an avenue for further secret surveillance, the squad of village elders is forced to enter:

At length, as it did not cease, and as there was no window on the side they stood, through which to reconnoitre [sic], the party was obliged to enter, in order to discover the cause of their alarm. The minister laid his hand on the latch—and the boldest deacon stood near to support him. They opened the door with the swiftness of lightening [sic], and stood before the astonished eyes of Margery.

Their sudden, uninvited appearance surprised her. But Margery Bethel showed "no dismay. Why should she? She was at the moment reading that consoling promise of the Saviour,—'Blessed are they that mourn, for they shall be comforted.'"

Both the cultural "logic" by which the merely unmarried Margery Bethel comes to be construed as a devil-worshipping witch, and the narrative logic by which the male authorities of Danvers are shown to have egregiously misread her, speak to the need for women's self-representation in the public realm. In the absence of a comprehensible story to explain and legitimize Margery's autonomous life, the community around her confabulates a phantasm with almost unending destructive potential. Silenced as to own her character and circumstances, Margery Bethel is construed as not merely wicked, but also monstrous. In contrast to the male "seducer" of Eliza's 1807 letter to the *Lady's Visitor*, who is transmogrified by his overt and unconscionable acts, Margery, omitted and storyless, is dangerous and inhuman because of the very absence of her story from the popular imagination.

The male authorities charged with containing this lurking peril on the margin of their town clearly lack the knowledge necessary to interpret and represent her. These pious men, pillars of their community, are so illiterate when it comes to women's stories that they misread the very text that authorizes them: they mistake the utterance of prayer for evil incantations. It is the female writer of the contribution who can reveal Margery's true character and narrate her circumstances. As the writer reveals Margery's story, exposing the inadequacies of the cultural authorities who license themselves to contain by interpreting her, she also subtly instructs her readers in the significant art of reading and writing—of self-possession and self-representation—as a woman. As a tale told by a woman's voice, Margery's life story becomes not only visible, but comprehensible and, by ascendant cultural standards, exemplary. Deserted by a recreant lover, and cruelly outcast by a community that ought to have embraced and protected her, Margery Bethel chose not to "rave" or plead desperately for help; neither was she ruined and defeated, becoming "cross" and "taciturn." Instead, she transcends the harm done to her in order to live out an emergent woman's plotline: hers is the story of an autonomous lady who leads a benevolent, pious life of her own.

Such narratives incorporate many of the strategies early women's magazine writers were using to subvert and redress the dominating idioms of male authority and authorship. Through the alternatives they made available, the collective work they determined to undertake, and the stories they soon dared to tell, contributors defeated the presumption of women's dutiful silence in public. By their methods as well as their messages, they also laid the groundwork—rhetorically, narratively, and socially—for an emergent vision of women's virtuous presence in the American public sphere. The next generation of readers further developed and endowed that vision of virtuous presence in the women's magazines of the early nineteenth century. And from there, anything could happen.

NOTES

1. This formulation depends on Jürgen Habermas, who conceptualizes the public as a discursive network through which reasonable parties, removed from private interests, could achieve consensus on public affairs. Jurgen Habermas, *The Structural Transformation of the Public Sphere* (trans. Thomas Burger, with Frederick Lawrence; Cambridge: MIT Press, 1989). See also Michael Warner,

The Letters of the Republic: Publication and the Public Sphere in Eighteenth Century America (Cambridge: Harvard University Press, 1990).

2. See Kenneth Cmeil, *Democratic Eloquence: The Fight Over Popular Speech in Nineteenth Century America* (New York: William Morrow and Company, 1990). On the literary marketplace, see Richard D. Brown, "From Cohesion to Competition" and Rhys Isaac, "Books and the Authority of Learning: The Case of Mid-Eighteenth-Century Virginia." Both in Joyce, Hall, Brown and Heinrich, eds., *Printing and Society in Early America* (Worcester: American Antiquarian Society, 1983). For women in public, see Glenna Matthews, *The Rise of Public Woman: Woman's Power and Woman's Place in the United States, 1630–1970* (New York: Oxford University Press, 1992) and Mary P. Ryan, *Women in Public: Between Banners and Ballots 1825–1880* (Baltimore: Johns Hopkins University Press, 1990).

3. See Caroline Garnsey, "Ladies Magazines to 1850: The Beginnings of an Industry," *Bulletin of the New York Public Library* 58 (1954), pp. 74–88. See also Bertha-Monica Stearns, "Before *Godey's*," *American Literature* 2 (1930), pp. 248–55.

4. Women's use of anonymity for self-defense is discussed by Joan DeJean, "Lafayette's Ellipsis: The Privileges of Anonymity," *PMLA* 99 (1984), pp. 884–902. The idea that the "letter's anonymity signaled its authenticity," which in turn served "as a marker of emotional femininity," is discussed by Katharine A. Jensen, "Male Models of Female Epistolarity; or, How to Write Like a Woman in Seventeenth-Century France." Some other discussions of the uses of anonymity are summarized in Elizabeth C. Goldsmith, "Authority, Authenticity, and the Publication of Letters by Women." The latter two articles are in Elizabeth Goldsmith, ed., *Writing the Female Voice: Essays on Epistolary Literature* (Boston: Northeastern University Press, 1989).

5. Patricia Okker, *Our Sister Editors: Sarah J. Hale and the Tradition of Nineteenth-Century American Women Editors* (Athens: University of Georgia Press, 1995), p. 8. See also Karen K. List, "Magazine Portrayals of Women's Role in the New Republic," *Journalism History* 13:2 (summer 1986), pp. 64–70.

6. The unsigned "Address on the Female Sex" is generally attributed to Paine, who edited the *Pennsylvania Magazine*.

7. Charles Brockden Brown, "The Rights of Women," *The Literary Magazine and American Register*, May 1805, as cited in Frank Luther Mott, *History of American Magazines, Vol. 1: 1741–1850* (New York: D. Appleton & Co., 1930), pp. 141–2.

8. See Karen K. List, "Magazine Portrayals of Women's Role in the New Republic," *Journalism History*, vol. 13, no. 2 (summer 1986), pp. 64–70.

9. Brown's aims are further complicated by subsequent turns in the dialogue, wherein the Lady asserts the justice of "admitting the female part of the community to elect and to be electible" [sic], while her appalled interlocutor thinks it sufficient that the happiness of women be "amply consulted." Brown, "The

Rights of Women," *Literary Magazine and American Register*, May 1805, as cited in Mott, *History of American Magazines, Vol 1: 1741–1850*, pp. 141–2.

10. The dynamics of epistolarity are treated by Janet Gurkin Altman, *Epistolarity: Approaches to a Form* (Columbus: Ohio State University Press, 1982). See also the essays collected by Goldsmith, ed., *Writing the Female Voice: Essays on Epistolary Literature*. Some useful insights into the letter as a mode of woman's expression and gendered silencing can be found in Elizabeth Heckendorn Cook, "Going Public: The Letter and the Contract in *Fanni Butlerd*," *Eighteenth Century Studies*, vol. 24 (fall 1990), pp. 21–45; and Blythe Forcey, "*Charlotte Temple* and the End of Epistolarity," *American Literature*, vol. 63, no. 2 (June 1991), pp. 225–41.

11. "Letters from a Brother to a Sister at Boarding School," *Ladies Magazine and Repository of Entertaining and Instructive Knowledge*, August 1792, pp. 167–72.

12. Ibid., October 1792, pp. 231–2.

13. "Ibid., pp. 232–4.

14. Ibid., November 1792, pp. 259–63.

15. See Nancy K. Miller, "Gender and Genre: An Analysis of Literary Femininity in the Eighteenth Century Novel" (Ph.D. diss., Columbia University, 1974).

16. Ann Douglas, *The Feminization of American Culture* (New York: Alfred A. Knopf, 1977).

17. For example, "LETTER from AMELIA to her HUSBAND," almost certainly *not* written by the dying Amelia, published in Gibbons's *Ladies Magazine and Repository of Entertaining and Instructive Knowledge*, August 1792, p. 142.

18. Cathy Davidson has described that in the first sentimental novels, "wife or mistress, woman's function was to be socially possessed or dispossessed . . . on the level of narration, the first [male-authored] American novel confirms female victimization." However, Davidson argues that female readers of these novels are expertly "seduced . . . not by their own uncontrollable desire but by the verbal chicanery of men. This masculine narrative superiority is part and parcel of the narrative method of [William Hill Brown's 1789 sentimental fiction] *The Power of Sympathy*. . . . Who, after all, would want to identify with Harriot, who has no surplus of identity to lend to another?" See Davidson, *Revolution and the Word: The Rise of the Novel in America* (New York: Oxford University Press, 1986), pp. 110–1.

19. The incompleteness of such narratives is underscored by Jane Tompkins's reading of the providential view that informs the sentimental formula in its mature form. She argues that the "narratives that lie behind [Susan Warner's 1851 best-seller] *The Wide, Wide World* are trials of faith—the story of Job and *Pilgrim's Progress*—spiritual 'training' narratives in which God is both savior and persecutor and the emphasis falls not on last-minute redemption, but on the toils and sorrows of 'the way.'" See Tompkins, *Sensational Designs: The Cultural Work*

of American Fiction 1790–1860 (New York: Oxford University Press, 1985), p. 183.

20. "The Beggar Girl," *Weekly Visitor, or Ladies' Miscellany*, November 19, 1803, p. 389.

21. Sympathy, "A Fragment," *Weekly Visitor, or Ladies' Miscellany*, February 12, 1803, p. 204.

22. "Sarah—A Fragment," *Weekly Visitor, or Ladies' Miscellany*, December 31, 1802, p. 101.

23. Kathryn Shevelow, "Fathers and Daughters: Women as Readers of the *Tatler*," in Elizabeth Flynn and Patrocinio Schweikart, eds., *Gender and Reading: Essays on Readers, Texts, and Contexts* (Baltimore: Johns Hopkins University Press, 1986), p. 107. Some useful discussions of patriarchal discourse in eighteenth-century British magazines for women include Kathryn Shevelow, *Women and Print Culture: The Construction of Femininity in the Early Periodical* (New York: Routledge, 1989); Peter John Miller, "Eighteenth-Century Periodicals for Women," *History of Education Quarterly* (fall 1971), pp. 279–86; Jean E. Hunter, "The *Lady's Magazine* and the Study of Englishwomen in the Eighteenth Century," in *Newsletters to Newspapers: Eighteenth-Century Journalism*. Papers presented at a Bicentennial Symposium at West Virginia University, March–April 1976.

24. Early Republican literature tells of many brothers and sisters in vexed relations. Charles Brockden Brown's novels, including *Weiland; or The Transformation, An American Tale* (1798) and *Memoirs of Carwin the Biloquist*, serialized in the *Literary Magazine* of Philadelphia between 1803 and 1805, amply demonstrate this preoccupation. See also Frank Shuffleton, "Mrs. Foster's Coquette and the Decline of Brotherly Watch," *Studies in Eighteenth-Century Culture*, vol. 16 (1986), pp. 211–24.

25. Davidson, *Revolution and the Word*, p. 20.

26. Davidson discusses that early American printers most often used what editorial interventions were available to them as a means of marketing and sales. "The printer's main business, in short, was to turn the author's manuscript into a salable commodity and then to sell it," she writes. Davidson, *Revolution and the Word*, p. 20.

27. See Ellen Fein and Sherri Schneider, *The Rules: Time Tested Secrets for Capturing the Heart of Mr. Right* (New York: Warner Books, 1999).

28. B., "Thoughts on Old Maids," *The Ladies Magazine and Repository of Entertaining and Instructive Knowledge*, July 1792, pp. 60–2.

29. *Weekly Visitor, or Ladies' Miscellany*, January 24, 1807, pp. 100–1.

30. Ibid., November 27, 1802, p. 60.

31. One of the earliest is in New York's *Lady's Weekly Miscellany*, April 3, 1803, p. 37.

32. For instance, "Female Heroism," in the *Weekly Visitor, or Ladies Miscellany*, January 29, 1803, p. 109; and "Female Heroism," in the *Weekly Visitor, or Ladies Miscellany*, July 21, 1804, p. 333.

33. "The Respect Due to Females," *Weekly Visitor, or Ladies Miscellany*, January 8, 1803, p. 108.

34. A Matrimonial Republican, "On Matrimonial Obedience." *Ladies' Magazine and Repository of Entertaining and Instructive Knowledge*, July 1792, p. 64–7.

35. Unfortunately, slavery is used in this way by contributors to a number of early women's magazine throughout the antebellum period—including some contributors to first- and second-generation feminist magazines, who at times deploy it with bitterness after black male suffrage alone was won.

36. Ruth-Ellen Boetcher Joeres and Elizabeth Mittman argue that a woman's use of the eighteenth-century essay form itself, with its "openness, its accessibility, its sense of initiated dialogue, its emphasis on the particular and the concrete, its stress on dynamic process" was in itself a subversive and transgressive act. See *The Politics of the Essay: Feminist Perspectives* (Bloomington: Indiana University Press, 1993).

37. The redefinition and evisceration of women's epistolarity is discussed by Katharine A. Jensen, "Male Models of Feminine Epistolarity"; by Elizabeth Goldsmith, "Authority, Authenticity and the Publication of Letters by Women"; by Patricia Meyer Spacks, "Female Resources: Epistles, Plot, and Power"; and by Susan K. Jackson, "In Search of a Female Voice: *Les Liaisons Dangereuses.*" In Allin Elizabeth Goldsmith, ed., *Writing the Female Voice: Essays on Epistolary Literature* (Boston: Northeastern University Press, 1989).

38. Discussing women's epistolarity in late-seventeenth-century Europe, Elizabeth Goldsmith acknowledges this understanding of the letter, noting that "over and over again we read that the female writing style is somehow particularly adapted to the epistolary form." The links between women's letters and self-expression in narrative form are explored by Patricia Meyer Spacks in "Female Resources: Epistles, Plot, and Power." Spacks's article, along with Goldsmith's "Authority, Authenticity and the Publication of Letters by Women," appear in Goldsmith, ed., *Writing the Female Voice: Essays on Epistolary Literature*.

39. An example is "SELECT LETTERS, or Specimens of FEMALE LITERATURE. LETTER 1. Lady Wortley Montague, to Lady—," *Ladies Magazine and Repository of Entertaining and Instructive Knowledge*, August 1792, pp. 38–40.

40. Eliza, "From a Young Lady to Her Seducer," *Weekly Visitor, or Ladies' Miscellany*, April 4, 1807, pp. 86–7.

41. Judith Fetterley, "Reading About Reading: 'A Jury of Her Peers,' 'The Murders in the Rue Morgue,' and 'The Yellow Wallpaper.'" See also Susan Schibanoff, "Taking the Gold Out of Egypt: The Art of Reading as a Woman." Both in Flynn and Schweikart, eds., *Gender and Reading: Essays on Readers, Texts, and Contexts*.

42. V., "The Criterion of Virtue," *Weekly Visitor, or Ladies' Miscellany*, November 20, 1802, p. 52.

43. "A New Trait in Female Character," *Ladies Magazine and Musical Repository*, May 1801, 292–4.

44. V., "Margery Bethel," (*American*) *Ladies' Magazine*, April 1828, pp. 170–4.

45. The sentimental-domestic formula arose in the 1830s and achieved literary prominence in the 1840s and 1850s. It is therefore treated in greater detail in my next two chapters. This reading of the genre's heroine is derived from Nina Baym's blueprint in *Woman's Fiction: A Guide to Novels by and about Women in America, 1820–1870* (Ithaca: Cornell University Press, 1978).

CHAPTER 4

Understanding Equals: Identity and Community in Sarah Hale's (American) Ladies' Magazine

In a July 1828 letter-to-the-editor in Sarah Hale's (*American*) *Ladies' Magazine* (1828–36),[1] an anonymous contribution introduces crucial, collective dynamics of the trend-setting magazine in which it appears. "I have heard someone observe," the contributor relates, "that an excellent way to ascertain our own character was to write the history of our own thoughts, feelings, and actions." Having reread her own diary entry recorded "one Sabbath Day," the writer fears that her sentiments might appear "too filled with levity." Obliquely, she then takes up the problem of Margery Bethel—and actual American women in all walks of life. Engaging the issue of woman's limited visibility and the cultural misrepresentation that results, she asks plaintively, "Will the world think me such a trifler?"

For the first time in periodical history, this woman has a place to go for the feedback she seeks. In submitting the entry to the magazine, she asks its community of women to help her reach self-judgment and a self-image with which to face the world. Given a responsive readership, she'll get it—and then some. Since Hale's magazine was the first American women's magazine to survive more than five years, the contributor would gain even more than feedback from women readers. Their ongoing participation and exchange could enable middle-class women to write their own role, their own story. Indeed, in this case, they worked to write their own destiny.

SEEING WOMEN CENTERED: SARAH HALE'S "WOMAN'S SPHERE"

Sarah Josepha Hale's editorial career was propelled by absences and loss. When she was hired to edit a ladies magazine by the principal of the

Cornhill School for Young Ladies in Boston, she was in desperate straits. Her whole life had taken a turn for the worse when on the same day in 1811 she lost both her mother and sister. Only a year later, her father's New Hampshire tavern went broke. Hale struggled through an economically strained adolescence, then married a promising attorney—only to lose him suddenly, and just four days after the birth of the couple's fifth child.

A young widow, alone, lacking the means to an income for her family of six, Hale took a flyer on the one job prospect she had. She packed up her children and moved to Boston to try to make a go of the new magazine. In light of these circumstances, it's not surprising that her initial marketing sought subscribers with a language of support. And given the controversial rise of the women's magazine, it makes sense that she appealed to the patriarchal concerns as well as the deep pockets of men.

Hale's introduction to the *Ladies' Magazine* in the January 1828 issue in fact seems to speak only to historically masculine interests, portraying the project as serving American fathers, brothers, husbands, and more obliquely, the nation itself. Fathers are assured that "nothing shall be found to weaken parental authority, or foster that fervor of imagination, which, when undisciplined by reading and reflection, often hurries youth . . . into the follies and extravagances that disturb family concord, and destroy domestic felicity."[2] Brothers would find relationships with their American sisters stabilized by the periodical. Hale promised they could "feel confident that the ties of kindred affection will be sacredly cherished, by the examples exhibited in this work." Husbands and lovers would also find the magazine useful, since it would help engender constancy: "The lover . . . will request her to gaze on that inconstant thing, the moon, so often obscured by clouds, and then remember her vows. He will present her with a subscription to the *Ladies Magazine;* and the sweet smile with which the gift is received, will recur."

A market-savvy wordsmith from the start, Hale quickly grasped the need to write to dual audiences. As the eventual author or editor of some fifty books—including two novels, children's books, etiquette guides, gift annuals, and several works of biography, most notably the *Woman's Record* (1853), an ambitious 2,500-entry encyclopedia of women's achievements—she clearly understood the fundamental recipe for success for a woman in her day: write for women while selling to men. Through her forty-year stint at the helm of the best-selling *Godey's Lady's Book* from 1837 to 1877,[3] Hale became identified with the discourse of domesticity, a set of beliefs about women that guaranteed great benefits to men, their presumed opposite and complement.

Domesticity has long been seen as simply the rationale for gender inequality, for female subservience and constraint. And at the launch of the *Ladies' Magazine,* Hale appears to conform, promising that her female readers will be recognized and reinforced as the helpmates of men. They will learn "not that they may usurp their station, or encroach on the prerogative of the man," she assures male patrons, "but that each individual may lend her aid to perfect the moral and intellectual character of those within her sphere." However, as Hale elaborates these patriarchal dicta, from the outset positioning women in the private realm of the home, and men, by multiple implication, in control from the public realm of everything else, her superficial entreaty to male patronage and power conveys an ulterior message.

Although Hale speaks to men and male concerns, she does so from a domestic, or culturally ascendant "feminine" perspective: men are construed in their familial and relational, rather than their political and individualist, character. Conventional masculine privilege might seem to be supported by her rhetoric, but the covert message is to subvert or reorganize men's cultural identity, and the privileges it has guaranteed, so as to serve women, home, and family. Domestic harmony and relational responsibilities are centered, whereas "masculine" authority and individual autonomy are marginalized. This transposition, and the re-valuation it both suggests and promotes, pulls men into a women's world, casting "feminine" authority, or at least a "feminine" perspective over all. That Hale's magazine "will be national—be American," and would be carried by the marketplace to an expanding readership, bespeaks the potential impact of this shift.

UNDERSTANDING EQUALS:
THE MAKING OF A WOMEN'S WORLD

Arising from her personal experience, Hale's true position seems to have been that women needed independence and strength—and that America needed these qualities from them. From the start, she constituted and continually supported a gender—and world—transforming environment in her magazine along these lines. For one thing, as a book reviewer, she gave visible endorsements to women authors.[4] And she structured her book reviews in ways that validated women readers' independent judgment. She offered "feminine" affirmative encouragement (and explicitly contrasted this approach with "masculine," dissective criticism): "I prefer giving directions where the young may find what will improve their minds and confirm in them the love of virtue," she notes in a July 1828 book review, "rather than occupy their time with disquisitions [sic] on the structure of sentences or the rhythm of poetry." Rather than to "discern and expose all the literary defects of every book," she typically chose to offer "a few extracts, from which may be gathered the spirit and tendency of the work." In the end, she hoped readers would "not rest satisfied, till they have examined and judged for themselves, of its character."

To this kind of structural support for women's independent thinking, Hale added directed encouragement to speak out about their own lives. She undertook specific editorial acts that pushed readers to become writers. A March 1829 "Letter to the Editor" sequence is just one example. A male writer with the initials "U.R."[5] had sarcastically submitted that "our good friends, the ladies, accuse our sex of frequently estimating things by their external appearance—because, on account of a certain affinity of taste, between the eye and the affections, a pretty woman charms us more easily, than one to whom nature has not been kind." The writer cannot "meet the charge with direct denial," but questions the one-sided susceptibility to a pretty face. His letter asks "whether the same accusation may not be justly made against our fair friends, which they so liberally heap upon us?"

U.R.'s story is as follows:

It was but the evening before, that I had met several . . . dear creatures, one of whom had twice been my partner in a cotillion. On the following morning . . . I encountered the three damsels abovementioned . . . and I prepared my most respectful, and at the same time, most sincere salutations. . . . But, just as I had uttered the sentence, 'good morning ladies,' or, 'your humble servant ladies' . . . I perceived to my utter astonishment and dismay, there was not the slightest sign of recognition on their part. [Later,] arriving at home, I was quickly re-appareled . . . [and] chance threw me in the way of these same fair friends. . . . I was noticed by a very familiar nod from one, a smile from the other, and a pretty loud salutation from the third.

Hale intercedes in this sequence, publishing a brief comment on U.R.'s letter.

"The Editor would suggest that an answer to U.R. by the young ladies alluded to in his epistle, would be very welcome to a place in the Magazine for next month. Women are never at a loss for reasons to justify their conduct; she therefore feels confident the affair will be explained entirely to the advantage of the ladies, and the insinuation, that they, like the men, are more "taken up with the outward appearance," than with "rational and sensible conversation," will be, with proper dignity, repelled.

The young readers did indeed write to the next issue. And they opened by acknowledging the value of Hale's encouragement to respond. "Mrs. Hale—had you not so kindly invited me (I am one of the young ladies mentioned by U.R.) in your last Magazine, to answer the curious epistle, I do not think I ever should have summoned resolution to appear in print."[6] So encouraged, the reader finds the strong conviction to assert that "luckily for me, no elaborate chain of reasoning is required to expose the absurdity of the conclusions drawn by my acquaintance, U.R." Promising to "tell the whole by-and-by," she first refutes U.R.'s ultimate charge: "no—neither the outward adornments nor the personal beauty of a man gains the favor of the ladies," she asserts. Instead, "it is the moral or mental qualities which we fancy the appearance indicates" that matters.

The once-hesitant young reader now writes strongly and at length that she is stupefied by "what a ridiculous story he made of that affair." At first calling upon "the authorities and examples of the respect for talents and genius which women have always evinced, sufficient to fill a pair of volumes as thick and heavy as Webster's American Dictionary," she then reveals her version of the story "that so discomposed the philosophy of Mr. U.R."

She writes that they were hurrying to Boston "with as much rapidity as if I had been the express to carry the President's speech," on a helping errand for her Aunt Jane. Having promised "not to speak [to anyone]" until they reached Boston, this in exchange for permission to travel with her two friends, the three dutifully discharged their assigned errand. And "by that means U.R. was offended." The contribution is signed with the young lady's Christian name—a change in the convention of anonymity-led antebellum women's magazines, especially Hale's[7]—"truly yours, LAURA."

U.R. had misread the situation, but perhaps reasonably so. Although not exactly in league with the negating brother, the omitting narrator, or Marjorie Bethel's town elders, he nevertheless fails to read or imagine the ladies' story. In the absence of that story, without recognition of the limits silently constraining it, he wrongly devises a pejorative reading. Given his privileged position within a culture that rarely rendered women's stories, how could he have read them right?

Hale's intervention is crucial for all concerned. She authorizes the women to reveal their obligation and its attendant promise, which answers U.R.'s accusation and vindicates them. For readers of the magazine, this sequence advances the idea that unfavorable attitudes about women's characters can result from cultural invisibility, from an inability on the part of the public to conceive and consider even their prescribed responsibilities, duties, and constraints, let alone their personal priorities or interests. The letters bring out the women's hidden story, righting these wrongs, for all the reading world to see.

Just as important, Hale's urging bolsters the young lady's daring, enabling them to enter the public space as speakers. Without the editor's strong and supportive presence, many women readers might never have become writers. Moreover, readers who are always-immanent writers make for the active audience ideally suited to capitalize on the constructive potential of the American magazine form.

Hale maintained a whole community of such active readers, a group that was crucial to the project of women's public visibility. The July 1828 letter that opens this chapter reveals a critical quality of that community. As we have seen, the contributor wonders aloud at her own "trifling" entries in her journal "one Sabbath day." She asks *Ladies' Magazine* readers to respond to her submission of the "unvarnished" version of her personal "history." Well versed in the Puritan ethic of self-examination and exposure that prevailed particularly in New England, she continues, "I cannot but think the effects of this exposure, this incognito, will be salutary."

The confessional urge of this contribution shares in what Jane Tompkins sees as the epitomizing conceit of the sentimental-domestic or "woman's" literary tradition of the antebellum era: an "ethic of submission."[8] As Tompkins argues, antebellum women writers who questioned or rejected the culture's value system nevertheless lacked means of opposition or escape; thus, following from the logic of popular religious tracts and exemplary narratives, Tompkins believes, they devised an empowerment structure based, like many biblical narratives, on reversal. In this context, a confession actually flouts external authority since, as Tompkins explains, the ethic of submission is "first of all a self-willed act of conquest of one's own passions." To command or compose oneself in this way, then, is an act of "mastery of herself, and therefore, paradoxically, an assertion of autonomy."[9]

From the beginning of the women's magazine tradition, writers have used all manner of logical and narrative reversals to enter and alter the power dynamics at play. Here, though, the position of readers is of interest. For this questioning contributor submits not to the male authorities of father, president, priest, or God, but instead to a collected group of other women magazine readers rather like herself, to a jury of her peers. This woman is engaged in a process of confession and self-exposure, as Tompkins discusses, but she does not invite the judgment of the male "external authorities" of the church or the state; rather, she requests feedback from an audience of understanding equals.

Hers is a complex revision of expectations, all with an egalitarian spin. The contribution is multiply an act of submission—literally of a contribution to the magazine, personally of her story to its women readers, and confessionally to them as well as to the reading public at large. And it is doubly an assertion of autonomy—in its consistency with Tompkins's paradox, and in its departure from its hierarchy of male authority. For in choosing to "submit" to the magazine, she rejects the female subservience embedded in the traditional exercise of submission. She shifts her dependence instead to an audience of women and of equals, leveling the very structure of feminine dependence itself. Thus, she alters but does not abolish the tradition in which she participates. By expressing a democratic preference for lateral collaboration among women over hierarchical obedience to men, she positions and empowers the magazine's readers—including herself—to act as the authors of their own public identities and powers. At least on paper.

SELF-MADE SAVIORS: THE WRITING WOMAN AS WORLDLY FORCE

Well, if communities of magazine participants, working actively together, could write their own identities—and revise the logic by which it was done—why couldn't they remake the whole male-dominated world?

It wasn't long before Hale's readers and writers together created a female figure to articulate this newfound sense of agency, independence, and self-determination. They incarnated a heroine who was not only made of discourse, but also espoused the power of language to remake the world. They conflated the salutary effects of women's writing with "feminine" mechanisms of maternal nurture and moral influence to invent the "writing woman heroine"—that is, an image of the writing woman as preeminent force for the public good. Having experienced successful discursive self-making and self-promotion in the magazine, they envisioned women's discursive agency as public power capable of accomplishing a range of national, indeed universal, goals. And such a self-reflexive heroine couldn't help but catch on. After all, contributors' own experiences in the magazine, and through it in the press-based public, confirmed the powers with which the writing woman heroine was endowed.

An early articulation of the idea of women's writing as worldly force appears in a letter-to-the-editor in the August 1828 issue. The letter describes the ascendancy of the woman's novel as an affirmation of the superiority of "feminine" values and influence.

Like Laura's letter about U.R, this missive is a response—but to the dominant, male-based and male-biased claim of literary nationalists that "patriotism inspires American literature."[10] The female contributor holds a markedly different set of meanings for literary acts. "Patriotism has nothing to do with the affair," she dashes. "Many of the articles [in magazines] are furnished from motives of private friendship, or benevolence, to encourage an individual in some favorite, or perhaps, necessary enterprise," she offers. "I understand the articles for the *Ladies' Magazine*, which have been contributed are offered . . . without expectation of reward."

The "masculine" motivators, here patriotism and profit, do not make sense to this female mind. But in America, what besides national pride or marketplace profit could inspire? The "consciousness of aiding one in need of assistance," she answers, celebrating the intangible rewards of "feminine" benevolence and service to others. "What delicate generosity!" she exclaims. Literary motivation, she then concludes, must be renamed and relocated to accord with the "feminine" sensibility. "We may truly call such acts," she writes, the outcomes of "exalted minds."

To this *Ladies' Magazine* contributor, writing and "patriotism" enact selfless service, not personal prowess. This "feminine" definition of national participation authorizes women to do it, and also "exalts" as superior their "patriotic" reasons for taking up the pen and the book. Men's baser motivations are obliquely denounced as being either animal, inhumane, or idiotic: men who write for fame or profit, apparently, do not have "exalted minds."

The magazine is seen by this contributor as a vehicle for the patriotic participation that women's words—including her own—connote. Although the publishing industry is nationalizing at this time, and American literary efforts (including some of Hale's) reflect the impulse for nationality building and national prestige, reading and writing are here conceived to profit the nation in utterly different terms. By suggesting that the literary enterprise demonstrates benevolence and support, the contributor elaborates a rationale for woman's participation in literary production and literary judgment that conforms to ascendant expectations of her sex. Collaboration and shared sentiment emerge as a viable mode, and benevolent service appears as an exalted rationale for women's entrance into literary production and public voice—with all its attendant cultural politics.

The transformative power of reading and writing, so justified and understood, is supported in the magazine by a cadre of contributions that increasingly and positively associate novel reading and novel writing with beneficial female influence to the wider culture. Another August 1828 contribution, "Novels," not only ascribes moral power to literary production and reception, but also raises this increasingly gendered force above "philosophy," a "masculine" mode. "The susceptibility of nature to be moved by example rather than precept"—or, by experience rather than expertise—is initially asserted by the anonymous contributor. This human tendency profoundly affects the power of certain kinds of literature to inspire and direct reading audiences. "The novel is, or may be, among the mightiest instruments for swaying the heart and guiding the lives of men," the writer believes. The heart here rightfully informs the head, and the novel, she writes, preeminently guides the heart. That women have a peculiar aptitude for both subtly suggests their power to "guide the lives of men."

"Novels and Novel Reading," an April 1828 contribution, similarly extends the constructive consequences of novel reading, and in markedly gendered terms. "Not many years ago, the word *novel* was charm to conjure up evil imaginations with, and the fathers and mothers of New-England started back and turned pale at the sound," the contributor begins.[11] Indeed, contemporary literary historian Cathy Davidson, among others, has borne this contributor out—and adds a twist. The elders of New England, Davidson argues, blanched at the novel's early association with women's understanding and self-expression.[12] Seeming to respond to the anxieties Davidson elucidates, the contributor asserts that an altered attitude toward the novel would be "a change for the better from a moral point of view."

"For the better" most likely means for a better world, and here that means one organized in women's terms. "Whatever may be the connexion [sic] between letters and moral purity," she continues, defending women's reading of the novel against its detractors, "they certainly open a never failing source of innocent gratification." The novel is as steady in its purposes as it is innocent in its pleasures, a claim that refutes patriarchal accusations of moral intoxication and surging appetite supposedly induced by reading them. The slippage given way in the novel's provision of "gratification" can hardly disrupt her sanctifying spin as she asks, "Who has not felt the healing influences of a good novel, when 'the whole heart has been sick, the whole head sore'?"

Novel reading is better than innocent; it actively heals. Better yet, it reforms, too. Novel reading, the writer suggests, can save the intemperate, a claim that, in the late 1820s, would have underscored the association between the effects of reading and writing and the salutary effects of female influence and activism: "How many men, had they known of this mental cordial, would never have sought relief in the bottle, at the hazard of life, health and respectability?" the contributor wonders.

If "innocent" novels can at times be corruptive to readers, this nefarious influence results from degenerate practitioners, here explicitly male producers of prose fiction:

Men of perverted taste and morals have ever abounded, who have been ready and willing to give up their pages for vice and folly . . . why should we expect that novel writing, the most popular of compositions, would remain unabused, when bad men have made the obscure details of grammar and philology, the grave speculations of science, even religion itself, the vehicles of their false sophisms, and loose morality?

Since men abuse their authority to speak, perverting the content of whatever they write to serve only their selfish sophisms while leading readers astray, women's benevolent motivations and aims are, by strong implication, superior, salutary, and necessary to check and to balance those tendencies.

If the desired cultural uplift is to be accomplished, this contributor continues, the popular novel's accessibility, and its "feminine" social graces, favorably appoint it to the task. "We . . . sink fondly down to the easy, unlabored, conversational style of the novel," she claims. Everybody loves an easy novel, she continues, asserting as a general rule its appeal to all readers, particularly men—who need the most elevating. "The higher poets choose subjects in which the generality of men feel little concern, and the loftiness of the heroic theme, if it adds dignity, diminishes interest," she asserts. "Compositions essentially didactic"—that is, "masculine" to the mind-set of Hale's magazine—"how artfully soever [sic] the writer may conceal the barrenness of his subject," she thinks, "must sometimes betray their inherent dulness." [sic]

The implicitly female novelist, by gendered contrast, "enters the wide and fruitful fields of domestic and social life." More relevant than the lofty "masculinism" of heroic tales or the dusty "dulness" [sic] of didactic narratives, women's writing is also more resonant, and, any way you slice it, more real. Women's writing, her rhetoric suggests, operates both naturally and culturally: it works the "fruitful fields" of "social life." Like motherhood, it has virtually limitless influence.

The "chief power" of women's writing emanates from its "feminine" subtlety. Its influence "lies in the development of those lesser and everacting motives which direct our daily conduct, so that our usual, every day feelings become the 'responsive strings of his minstrelsy.'" Despite this contributor's use of the masculine pronoun "he" to describe the novelist, the claim of the novel's capacity to "soothe," references to its insight into "social life," "lesser and ever-acting motives," and "every day feelings," and the suggestion that novel reading awakens one's heart to God's "minstrelsy" all encode the socially saving novel as a "feminine" form. The "mental cordial" of the novel, "a luxury, like every other luxury, [that] ought to be temperately indulged in," this Victorian lady cautions, is nevertheless a beneficent cultural influence. It "successfully stud[ies] the human heart" to "exert all the good influences on the mind, the heart and the feelings," like the image of woman herself, in a "universal and prevailing" way.

This capacity to study, "minutely and faithfully," the interior workings of the heart is made an explicit attribute of "Female Character" in an issue published right in between the two previous pieces. In a May 1828 contribution, the writer contends that woman's keen perception of interior worlds—a definitive quality of domestic writing[13]—justifies men's subordination *to her* and her inevitable rise to a superior status. Women "have long been the acknowledged possessors of a sort of mental quickness and intellectual acumen, or rather sharpness of vision . . . which has enabled them to discern, or at least to recognize those smaller springs of action that regulate the conduct of mankind," she asserts, "which from their supposed insignificancy [sic], have escaped the notice of the grosser sex."[14]

Published just two months later, in July 1828, the same writer contributes "Female Influence," which carries the now-shared qualities of women and writing explicitly into the public sphere. Women's "peculiar ability for any kind of benevolent love," also a stated aspect of their reading and writing, renders them superior in public works.[15] "Men may have tender feelings," the writer submits, but the world of competition apparently inhibits, effaces, or perverts them. Although she does not enumerate the particular failings that result from "masculine" competition, the contributor strongly implies them by her articulation of women's superjacent qualities. In fact, woman is here rendered in heroic terms:

Towards the softer sex there is no obstacle to the full exercise of benevolent affections—that like the concealed fire in the bowels of the earth must vent the strong sympathies which characterize the sex and lead them warmly to espouse the views which are taken by the objects of their peculiar interest and enable them also to direct and control the ardour of pursuit when it is difficult or dangerous. There is no suspicion of rivalry, no fear of envy, no dread of enmity, no anxiety for the continuance of a pure and steadfast affection.

Woman is a sleeping volcano, whose "benevolent affections" are again both a natural and a cultural force. Although this woman operates in the passive voice—she is led by "strong sympathies" to act—her inner light, here a "concealed fire," compels her to "espouse views." Such motivation both forgives and makes necessary her public activism.

Rebutting the prevailing notion that women's "peculiar abilities" make them unreliable leaders, or impossible heroes, this contributor articulates the early blueprint for feminine heroism. The contributor counters prevailing stereotypes about woman's weakness, frivolity, and inconstancy by invoking a goal-oriented emotional commitment that is "directed and controlled," even in the face of physical "difficulty or danger." The contributor puts forth a new image of woman, clearing her way by an old strategy: negation. But she negates negatives—*no* suspicion; *no* envy; *no* enmity; *no* rivalry; *no* fear; *no* dread; *no* anxiety—a context that lets her open rather than foreclose possibilities.

As the contributor proceeds to rebut male-authored stereotypes of women, she puts male flaws in their stead. The "allegation that woman is fickle or inconstant in her affections has no foundation in truth," the writer argues. "Her feelings it is true are ductile, and docible," [*sic*] she explains, but such adaptability is woman's signal strength. "The affections of woman also may be drawn from her home, her kindred, or her country, to twine themselves about any deserving object that courts their embrace," she asserts. "Moral strength, power and influence . . . is not only the compensation made for the denial [of physical strength], but it has a higher and holier effect." The sources of woman's strength are multiple—as are its implied applications. Woman's benevolent feeling may be fired by her home, her family, or her nation, and its "higher and holier effect"—higher and holier, that is, than men's power and influence—will be felt anywhere she chooses to apply it.

BENEVOLENCE UNBOUND: WRITING WOMEN REVISING THE WORLD

This "writing woman heroine" helped Hale and her readers see their discursive action as models of influence for everywoman and the world. The collective and self-reflective qualities of the heroine rendered her at once more available to ordinary women readers and more vulnerable to individual vagary and error, to disruption and change. This is not to say that readers took the ideas or directives of what was a partial prototype of sentimental-domestic womanhood lightly or incompletely. Quite the contrary. The very intensity of contributors' faith in emergent domestic discourse, the heightened emotional investment that marked it, also made way for its undoing.

A righteous conviction in the premises and promises of this new brand of womanhood sometimes encouraged amateur writers to overreach. One dizzying contribution after another evacuates domesticity's immanent politics for poetics. Leaving behind (and below) an implicit critique of "masculine" and marketplace domination, contributors' abstract vision and mediated methodology risks re-inscribing the public passivity and practical remove of its primary agents: women.

However, although contributors to the *Ladies' Magazine* rarely articulated an awareness of this evanescent turn of mind, they did confront it— together. Contributions tended to evaporate at crucial moments, instigating subsequent contributors to fill in newfound gaps, or pick up where sister contributors seemed to gasp, lapse, or lose their way. Ironically, the tendency toward dissipation at key moments inspired, and the magazine's climate and long life enabled, the collective development of discourse that went further than any one contributor probably would have gone alone.

Readers' ongoing interaction on the subject of female authorship is a case in point. A December 1828 contribution, titled "Authoresses," deploys a string of discourses—anything and everything made available to her through the magazine's miscellaneous content—to argue for educational opportunity for American women. But as the contributor progresses, she pushes beyond her own terms, opening the way for subsequent contributors to take up the case (with all due benevolent service in mind) and press on.

The writer begins using spatial language that suggests woman's exclusion and her lowly status in many fields of American life. She then boldly contends that should woman "no longer be considered an intruder in the fields of science, [and] be permitted to take an honorable seat in the temple of learning," this eventuality will "not only [permit] much of the happiness and permanent respectability of my own sex, but it will, also, materially affect the happiness and order of society, and even the character of our country."[16]

Changing tacks, the writer moves from an educated citizenry to government and public policy. "It should always be borne in mind that our form of government is dependent on public opinion," she begins, and then spins "that this public opinion is only the expression of a majority of private opinions, and that if the majority of our citizens are not honest, and

well instructed in the knowledge of their rights and duties, our republican institutions will surely become corrupted." Although the writer ultimately stresses the importance of an educated "majority"—which, of
course, must presume the inclusion of women in government process—
her overall claim depends on the role of "public opinion," a factor over
which women are widely seen to exercise particular "influence."

The contributor is writing politically, but within a "feminine" frame.
She sees democracy, the formal "order" of American society, as depending on individuals whose learning is more personal, experiential, and
"feminine" than the learned individualism elaborated in male-authored
political documents of the period. Not only does this writer's "majority"
actually include at least both (white) men and women, but these collected
citizens rule by a different kind of popular sovereignty, by public opinion,
a collective force far more amenable to "feminine influence" than, for
example, the law or even the vote.

America's aspiring "republican institutions" will be assured, then, so
long as they fall under woman's jurisdiction. "Not the enlightening of the
minds of the people merely," she elaborates, "but the culture of the heart,
the discipline of the passions, the regulation of the feelings and the affections are important in [their] consequences [and should] never be committed to incompetent or inferior agents."

Having volleyed from institutional governing to cultural mothering, creating a viable link between them, the writer then covers her flank. She
stops to attach a patriarchal rationale for safekeeping. "What father," she
asks, "wishing his children to be wise and good, would willingly entrust
them . . . to an ignorant or a feeble minded person?" Now located firmly
on familial grounds, the writer justifies educational equity using more
explicitly private and emotional rhetoric. She sounds like a classic domestic speaker: "may not most of the ignorance and consequent misery of
mankind have suffered be traced to the early neglect and undervaluing
of the agents by whom this early training has been carried on?" Pushing,
characteristically, from family to infinity, she elevates the importance of
her claim, belying woman's lowered status and transcending those early
metaphors of constricted and restricted space.

Having traveled from politics to public opinion, to parenting, to eternity, the contributor finally turns to the discourse of history. And it is this
discourse that she apparently aims to change. "For nearly 6000 years has
the female intellect been suffered to remain a blank, either neglected or
derided," the writer declares. "No wonder the *few* who escaped such
thraldom sometimes use the liberty of their faculties unguardedly, improp-

erly, even dangerously, if you will, to the happiness of their own families, perhaps even to the disturbance of society," she asserts. But the writer does not let stand even her own account of some women's failings. She does not accept that precedent as predictive.

Instead, she looks ahead, arguing that a few of women's past wrongs do not justify all women's future punishment. "The abuse of reason does not prove that women have no use for reason," she writes. "Neither does the *little* they have as yet ostensibly contributed to the stock of general knowledge demonstrate that they are incapable of such exertion, or that it would be, under different circumstances," she ventures yet further, "overstepping the modesty and privileges of their sex, should they actually become co-workers with the lords of creation in the fields of science and national improvement."

This contribution pivots from discourse to discourse as the writer tries to find her position, her place, amidst the two rationales for women's entry into the public that dominated nineteenth-century debates. Would the "national housekeeper" argument take her where she wants to go, or does she come down closer to the claim that all Americans are created equal? Searching for language and creating new links, she finally arrives at the perhaps unforeseen conclusion that equal education ought to lead to gender equality in America. With the education they rightfully deserve, she ultimately concludes, women will enter as "co-workers" the markedly masculine domains of "science" and "national improvement." Yet, the contributor posits, this equality on earth can occur without "overstepping the modesty" or complicating the pedestal "privileges" that at least some women enjoyed. This utterly revised (or rescued) culture, that is to say, can happen without disrupting the established order of things. Taking care to acknowledge the requisite station of nineteenth-century "femininity," the contributor is stopped short of imaging just how these "different circumstances" ought to be realized. Just as the writer supposes this equal participation, "femininity" stymies her argument.

Critically, the apparent conflict between the imperative of women's education and public participation, on the one hand, and the gendered injunction against "overstepping the modesty and privileges of their sex," on the other, remains unresolved in the contribution. In fact, the writer's preview of this resolution is written in perplexed prose so conflicted and uncomfortable as to be ungrammatical and barely comprehensible. "How this [resolution] may be accomplished," the writer begins, "without endangering in the least the supremacy in all that properly belongs to the government of the earth—which, believing as I do, that it was by the

Almighty delegated expressly to the man, (mark me, not deserved by any superior strength of mind, except what may be derived only from the superior strength of physical powers,) I have no wish to controvert or undervalue—I shall in my next number attempt to show." Even this promised demonstration, however, never truly appears in the magazine.

The March 1829 submission, "An Authoress—No. II," instead recants and then recasts the cultural ramifications of the earlier number, asserting that "attempts to inspire women with an ambition to appear like men"—presumably a reference to the coworkers proposition—is too absurd to merit discussion."[17] Rewriting, the contributor still advances, but euphemistically, in poetics, that "there is no country where the right direction of female influence is so necessary as in America, because here the popular breath guides, as it were, the bark of the State." The cockeyed quality of this image—does breath guide a bark, or give it its power?—expresses a good deal about the problematic place from which she is trying to speak. Owing to the pitfalls of this political territory into which the writer has moved, she ultimately settles on the limited contention that "females might be extensively employed in school-keeping." Although this professional opportunity for women promoted improvement in their cultural status, it falls far short of the vastly "changed circumstances" and their participation as "co-workers" raised in the earlier contribution.

In the three-month lapse between the publication of the two versions, however, readers' own views about the vital possibilities broached here were formally and intellectually obliged. Subsequent contributions to the *Ladies' Magazine* suggest that such independent thinking about women's equal intellectual opportunity was, in fact, instigated by "Authoresses." In the next number, April 1829, "The Intellectual Character of Woman" begins at the question of "different circumstances": "Whoever will be at pains to reflect, for a moment, upon the very different means of education hitherto enjoyed by the two sexes, must be constrained to acknowledge, that the result of each must necessarily be widely different," the writer asserts. Before any discussion of abilities or roles can begin, she writes, "it must be recollected that few have enjoyed the mutual advantages necessary to produce . . . equality."[18]

Condensing the political and the spiritual discourses employed by the first two paragraphs of "Authoresses" into one, this submission, by "R.G.P.," expands the parameters of the earlier article. R.G.P. reorganizes the question, in fact, ingeniously arguing that the "changed circumstances" must be realized before the question of superiority and inferiority can be addressed. "We must not institute comparison between those of one sex, who are within the temple of science, and those of the other, to whom the doors have been closed," she argues.

Instead, we must offer them equal opportunity, placing men and women on equal footing at the base of a great mountain headed—where else?— upward toward heaven and the light. Here poetics supports gender politics. "We must lead them both to the steep ascent. We must observe their progress with vigilance," the contributor insists. But the writer turns and then envisions a broadening and opening of opportunity that can be seen from that altitude. "We must give to each the same advantages of birth and fortune; the same opportunities for intellectual culture. . . . We must open to each indifferently the halls of academic learning; of judicial science and legislative wisdom . . . before the question of the intellectual inferiority can be completely and satisfactorily settled."

R.G.P.'s final paragraph, having contended with increasingly evanescent imagery "the absolute natural equality of the intellectual character of the two sexes," nevertheless moves, like "Authoresses" before her, toward recontainment. Interestingly, in precisely the same terms that the anti-suffrage press later used, the contributor retracts somewhat her claims to equality outside the home for fear of relinquishing newly acquired domestic authority.[19] "We hope that the day is far distant when the question is to be decided in the manner we propose," she notes, for "we fear that the attempt, on the part of the gentle sex, to establish equality, would be attended with loss, greater than the acquisition of their aim." The fear that actual possibilities will fall short of imagined ones haunts many contributors of this period and beyond it. The sense that opening one door closes another, that women's choices are severely restricted and penalties for gains are high, conditions the claims as well as the structure of women's writing in magazines throughout at least the nineteenth century.[20] All but the most radical writers—and some of them—submit long articles or series pressing for only a single revision or right, and they often purvey these limited demands in accredited language and on conventionally gendered grounds.

Nevertheless, women's magazine contributors continue to fill in the gaps opened by one another's articles, pressing forward inch by inch by inch from the point at which evaporation or retraction occurs. Another subsequent contribution, "Man's Mental Superiority Over Woman, Referrible [sic] To Physical Causes Only" by "N.L.," (August 1829), takes up the case of intellectual equality explicitly where "Authoresses" left off. This writer resolves the problem of argumentative evaporation in both a conservative and a trend-setting way. She employs consistently the spiritual or transcendent rhetoric of the final, dizzying paragraph of "Authoresses," reserving her social claims for an addendum attached at the end.

Using religious rhetoric, this contributor asserts the equality of women and men in the eyes of God, writing that "Woman, 'the last and best of all create' was made also in the image of her Creator."[21] From there, her rhetoric plays with the relative position of the sexes, adjusting their status along a vertical field that extends from heaven to earth. Woman "was endowed with powers of mind as sublime, as exalted as those of the proud monarch of this lower world," she continues, but it is man's brutality, his baseness—not women's weakness—that has caused the observable imbalance in their status: "From the very delicacy of her nature, which constitutes her glory," the writer argues, lifting woman up, "she was appointed by her Maker to look to man for protection," since he is "gifted with mightier *physical* energies."

Just as in novel writing, though, "masculine" infractions, not "feminine" frailties, are to blame for gender inequity. "Beneficial intentions of Heaven have in this instance, as in numberless others, been frustrated by the pride, presumption and passions of men," she writes. "He who was created to be woman's defense, her shield, glorying in his superior animal strength, has looked up to himself as her lord and master, and down upon her as an inferior being."

"But," she halts, repositioning herself and her argument along a horizontal plane suggestive of social progress, "thanks to the advance of truth, the time will come, if it has not already come, when woman, exerting her powers with which God has endowed her, will assert her rights and stand forth side by side on perfect mental equality with the self-styled lords of creation."

This contributor's structure is just as important as her language. The concluding sentence, proceeding from the ominous exception, "but," signals a discursive shift that will bring a new tone and trajectory to her piece. The prediction (and warning) that equality's "time will come" is put forward in a closing paragraph that is structurally discrete. And in that space, the contributor steps outside herself, speaking more directly to her audience than in the preceding material. This addendum is a kind of rider, and one that presages social change as it also establishes an explicit discursive space for the author to predict or describe it.

This structural device, about which we will hear more in the next chapter, helps the writer maintain her domestic decency while making an overtly political point. It formally distances her from the public criticism she is articulating. Coupled with her general deployment of religious rhetoric, language widely accredited for women's use, the device permits the contributor to "stand forth side by side with perfect mental equality" to men, without hesitation, evaporation, or subsequent retraction.

STANDING FORTH SIDE BY SIDE: COLLECTIVE BENEVOLENCE AND THE ADVANCE FROM HOME TO WORLD

As these middle-class women proceed—two steps forward, one step back—to read and write themselves into cultural authority and gender efficacy, their contributions assiduously promote the value of their brains, their perspectives, their voices. Still, the public woman envisioned here wields only *representational* democracy. Her power remains largely imaginative and almost fully discursive. The next generation of women's magazine writers began to realize the practical power of making and manipulating public images, but (*American*) *Ladies' Magazine* contributors seem to have been writing themselves back out of the new picture of America they meant to paint.

However, it is crucial to recall that in this era, contributors would have understood their discursive action as akin to, if not identical to, public activism. Not only had the women's magazine long been draped in democratic garb and its public status affirmed by the various cultural accomplishments of the press since colonial times, but also, closer to home, the very practice of reading and writing were believed by antebellum audiences to exist on a continuum with personal action. As Nina Baym explains, "the novel, in a basic sense, existed only when the distinction between it and the reader disappeared, when the novel initiated and the reader completed a single experience."[22] These understandings, generally available in popular print culture and made more apparent to women readers through their own experiences in growing numbers of women's magazines, justify their faith in the actual power of the women's discursivity—even if history would not make all their dreams come true.

The belief in the kinship of literature to life did carry some women visibly from discursive heroics to actual public action. The August 1828 contributor who wrote "Intemperance," for example, believes in the writing of woman's cultural power in a direct and practical way. "Female influence has been so clearly demonstrated," the writer begins, "that it now appears only necessary to determine the particular direction in which influence would be most beneficial."[23]

Proceeding carefully so as not to overtly step outside the boundaries of middle-class femininity, she disclaims, "I disdain all intention of writing politically," querying "what business has a lady's paper with politics?"

Whatever responses this open query might have instigated among readers, the contributor answers tellingly. She makes a directed contrast to
established, "masculine" approaches to politics, suggesting that, in fact,
"writing politically" is exactly what she wishes she could do. "Arms and
physical courage are here of no avail," she writes, "—nor can reason be
relied on as a defense to those who most confidently boast its possession."
Instead, the logic of the popular is again entwined with "feminine" influence and invoked as politics. Social problems "can only be conquered
by the efforts of public opinion, and this opinion is guided materially by
the feelings, and taste and sentiments of ladies," she asserts.

The contributor then articulates the merger of women's self-created cultural image with her "feminine" cultural duty to enact the virtues it carries
in the service of cultural change. Here discourse conditions experience;
text is expected to initiate an actual, lived response:

Here is a glorious theater for the display of all feminine perfections; —patience
prudence, perseverance; softness; energy; gentleness and fortitude; that firmness
that yields not to example or entreaty, and the meekness that boasts not its own
conquests; the high-souled purity that disdains alliance with vice, however fashionable, and the tenderness that weeps the victims of an insidious temptation;
the hope that never despairs while there is duty to be performed, and the faith
that never wavers while there is a promise of God on which to rely.

This contribution puts the heroism of the writing woman in the realm
of "real" American life. The "glorious theater" is a perfect metaphor since
both discursive vision and "real" enactment operate within it. Like
Andrew Bradford's use of the theater image for the American magazine
as a form, this iteration similarly suggests a level of remove from politics,
while also authorizing and encouraging women to make an entrance. This
would appear, then, to be one of the discursive moments for which the
American magazine for women was both born and made.

"Ladies, if you have this influence," the writer exhorts in an authorial
addendum, "exert it and banish the demon of intemperance from among
us." As is characteristic with this closing device, she speaks directly to her
audience, here a group of women very much aware of the interests at stake:
"Achieve that task and female influence will never more be denied or derided." With that final sentence, this contributor invites women not necessarily morally directed to enter cultural politics side by side with others,
for reasons of their own.

Even if many aspects of the domestic vision seem to have set women
up for more than a century of struggle for political change, for true public

inclusion, history suggests that the participatory processes facilitated by magazines such as Hale's may have prompted numbers of middle-class women readers to own the image—and answer its discursive call. For all its self-imposed prohibitions, restrictions, and logical complications, the discursive heroism elaborated in Hale's (*American*) *Ladies' Magazine* likely inspired an early band of American women to move out of the home and into the wide, wide world.

NOTES

1. The magazine had several different titles during its eight-year run. It began as the *Ladies' Magazine*; between 1830 and 1833 it became the *Ladies' Magazine and Literary Gazette*; for one issue (January 1834), it returned to the *Ladies' Magazine*. Beginning in February 1834, and continuing until Louis Godey bought it in late 1836, it was the *American Ladies' Magazine*.

2. [Sarah Hale], "Introduction," (*American*) *Ladies' Magazine*, January 1828, pp. 1–3.

3. Hale's first book of verse, *The Genius of Oblivion* (1823), was said to reveal her sense of loss after her husband's death. Her *Poems for Our Children* (1830) was written, as Hale notes in her preface, "literally with a baby in my arms." These literary efforts attracted notice and soon led to her editorship of the *American Ladies' Magazine*. While Hale struggled to make a profit with the magazine (between 1834 and 1836, she also edited the *Juvenile Miscellany*), publisher Louis Godey invited her to become editor of his women's magazine, *Godey's Lady's Book* (1830–98). She accepted in 1836, producing her first issue of *Godey's* in January 1837. The magazine's circulation broke all records under her leadership, soaring to a reported 150,000 subscribers by 1860. While editing the 100-page best-selling monthly, Hale also wrote or edited some fifty books, including *Traits of American Life* (1835), a collection of local-color vignettes about American personalities, and *Woman's Record* (1853), a biographical encyclopedia containing more than 2,500 entries intended to remedy the neglect of women's works in history. Biographies of Hale include Ruth E. Finley, *The Lady of Godey's* (Philadelphia: J.B. Lippincott, 1931); Isabelle Webb Entrikin, *Sarah Josepha Hale and Godey's Lady's Book* (Philadelphia: J.B. Lippincott, 1946); Sherbrooke Rogers, *Sarah Josepha Hale: A New England Pioneer* (Grantham, N.H.: Tompson & Rutter, 1985); Olive Woolley Burt, *First Woman Editor* (New York: Messner, 1960); Patricia Okker, *Our Sister Editors: Sarah J. Hale and the Tradition of Nineteenth-Century Editors* (Athens: University of Georgia Press, 1995).

4. Hale's Literary Notices endorse "Miss Sedwick's Novels" (May 1828) and Mrs. Carey's abolitionist writings, among many others. A rich discussion of Hale's literary taste, style, and criticism is in Patricia Okker, *Our Sister Editors*.

5. U.R., "Letter to the Editor," (*American*) *Ladies' Magazine*, March 1829, pp. 135–8. Hale's note appears immediately after the close of U.R.'s letter, p. 138.

The double entendre here raises the possibility that the sequence is a setup to get the women involved and that "U.R." (or "you are") is a cover for Hale herself.

6. Laura, "Letter to the Editor" (American) Ladies' Magazine, April 1829, pp. 184–6.

7. Hale herself, as editor of Godey's, was a leader in this call. The use of bylines became standard industry practice during the 1870s. See Frank Luther Mott, American Journalism: A History of Newspapers in the United States Through 250 Years (New York: Macmillan, 1941).

8. See Jane Tompkins, Sensational Designs: The Cultural Work of American Fiction 1790–1860 (New York: Oxford University Press, 1986), particularly chapter 6.

9. Tompkins, Sensational Designs, p. 162.

10. "To the Editor of the Ladies' Magazine," (American) Ladies' Magazine, August 1828, pp. 370–2. Frank Luther Mott notes that when it comes to explaining why American magazines were attempted despite unfavorable conditions, "there was at least one other motive quite as effective as hope of profit, and that was the desire to show America favorably to the world, and especially to England." See Mott, A History of American Magazines, Vol. 1: 1741–1850 (New York: D. Appleton and Company, 1930), p. 22.

11. Colimetis, "Novels and Novel-Reading," (American) Ladies' Magazine, April 1828, pp. 145–7.

12. Cathy Davidson, Revolution and the Word: The Rise of the Novel in America (New York: Oxford University Press, 1986).

13. "Domestic fiction was . . . associated with women because they were supposed to have the finer powers of observation and discrimination that the minute chronicling of domestic detail required for interest or notice." Nina Baym, Novels, Readers, and Reviewers: Responses to Fiction in Antebellum America (Ithaca, NY: Cornell University Press, 1984), p. 206.

14. P., "Female Character," (American) Ladies' Magazine, May 1828, pp. 192–201.

15. P., "Female Influence," (American) Ladies' Magazine, July 1828, pp. 289–94.

16. "Authoresses," (American) Ladies' Magazine, December 1828, pp. 30–4.

17. "An Authoress—No. II," (American) Ladies' Magazine, March 1829, pp. 130–4.

18. R.G.P., "The Intellectual Character of Woman," (American) Ladies' Magazine, April 1829, pp. 146–50.

19. Four extant periodicals make up the known anti-suffrage press: True Woman (1850–4), The Anti-Suffragist (1908–??), Woman's Protest (1912–8), and Woman Patriot (1918). An extensive bibliography of antifeminist writing is Cynthia Kinnard, Antifeminism in American Thought: An Annotated Bibliography (Boston: G.K. Hall, 1986).

20. Indeed, Susan Faludi's argument suggests that women's gains have continued to be accompanied by a "backlash" of meaningful losses or other penalties. See Faludi, *Backlash: The Undeclared War Against American Women* (New York: Crown, 1991).

21. N.L., "Man's Mental Superiority Over Woman, Referrible to Physical Causes Only," *(American) Ladies' Magazine*, August 1829, pp. 367–71.

22. Baym, *Novels, Readers, and Reviewers*, p. 81.

23. Censor, "Intemperance," *(American) Ladies' Magazine*, August 1828, pp. 337–40.

CHAPTER 5

Media Makeovers: Converting the Popular to Politics in America's First Feminist Magazines

In a late, year-end issue of America's very first feminist magazine, the *Lily* (1849–58), a December 1856 contribution captures a critical moment in the evolution of woman's public image in the nineteenth century, a moment made possible by the magazine itself. The writer, Jane Frohock, proclaims, "It is woman's womanhood, her instinctive femininity, her highest morality, that society now needs to counteract the excess of masculinity that is everywhere to be found in our unjust and unequal laws."[1]

The contributor uses the ideological touchstones of domesticity, the popular gender discourse of her day, to pursue feminist politics.[2] Her footing is grounded on the idea of woman's instinctive "morality," a cardinal claim, and she moves, phrase by phrase, through another prevailing idea: "femininity" is seen as the necessary corrective to male dominance of the public, law-making domain. Frohock's sentiment reads like textbook domestic discourse except for its direct object; here, "womanhood" explicitly targets the law. Two conflicting gender discourses—"feminine" and feminist—cooperate rather than compete. They form a sequence of assertions that both propels and sustains the writer's call for political change.

The discursive development on which this transformation depends was promoted by the *Lily*'s formal qualities and periodical practices, particularly at the moment in periodical history when the magazine was produced. As we have seen, the American magazine functioned in cultural practice as a forum, providing a space for the rhetorical and ideological exchange through which new language, new images, new stories could—and did—emerge. The first American feminist magazines of the 1850s put participating women in a perfect position, both formally and historically, to work on popular gender discourse. Their various dynamics and discursive properties helped "women's rights women" push the popular to tell a different story.

THE FEMINIST MAGAZINE: GENDER POLITICS AND PERIODICAL HISTORY

The earliest American feminist magazines, a group of seven national players, were part of a small but recognizable tradition of reform journalism in the United States.[3] In addition to the *Lily*, there was the intellectual and policy-oriented *Una* (1853–55), a sixteen-page monthly edited by Paulina Wright Davis and Caroline Healy Dall in Providence, Rhode Island. The *Pioneer and Women's Advocate* (1852–53), Anna W. Spenser's four-page semimonthly, was also published near Providence. The *Genius of Liberty* (1851–53) was an eight-page monthly edited by Elizabeth Aldrich of Cincinnati, Ohio, and the only one of the group to refuse advertising on principle. The *Woman's Advocate* (January 1855–58 or 1860), Anne McDowell's Philadelphia monthly, was written, edited, printed, and sold exclusively by women. The *Sibyl* (1856–64), edited by Dr. Lydia Sayer Hasbrouk of Middletown, New York, began as a dress reform magazine, but soon expanded its scope beyond that single-issue focus. The *Mayflower* (1861–64?), an eight-page semimonthly published by Lizzie Bunnell in Peru, Indiana, was the only one of the feminist magazines to publish during the Civil War years.[4]

The *Lily*, the longest-lived of its generation, was an eight-page monthly edited until 1855 by Amelia Bloomer, most of that time in Seneca Falls, New York. Bloomer was not a professional journalist.[5] Like her sister editors of the first feminist magazines, she became a movement leader. In fact, it was her experience with the *Lily* that helped take her there.

The *Lily* began in January 1849 "Devoted to Temperance and Literature." But by the early 1850s, Bloomer had discovered that the issue of temperance led to a broader debate about women's rights. Working as she was in the birthplace of American feminism, she began printing articles by some radical and outspoken women writers, including the first published work of Elizabeth Cady Stanton (in April 1850). Soon she ran three illustrated editorials endorsing the "Bloomer costume" (in July 1851, and two in September 1851). Bloomer suffered intense ridicule as a result of the editorials, and these jibes included the pejorative naming of the Turkish-style pants outfit after her. Such content and controversy was too much for the Female Temperance Society that was footing the bill for the magazine, and the organization soon withdrew its financial support.

Unbowed, Bloomer began editing and publishing the magazine on her own in April 1852. Now carrying the motto "Devoted to the Interests of Women," the *Lily* was open to a generic range of contributions—short stories, letters, essays, some poetry, reportage, reviews, and various kinds of fragments—all concerning emergent issues in women's rights. It is remarkable that the magazine's topical content is not that distant from the modern-day *Ms.*: the gender of poverty, women's employment, absent fathers, domestic tyranny, and women's political enfranchisement dominated its pages.[6] A subscription sold for a low $.50 per year, and that amount did not change even after the *Lily* began publishing biweekly in 1853 or after it resorted to semimonthly publication in 1855. By that time, Bloomer had sold the *Lily* to a Richmond, Indiana, literary lady, Mary B. Birdsall, a former editor of the Ladies' Department of the *Indiana Farmer* (1851–61). Although Bloomer stayed on as corresponding editor through December 1856, the *Lily* became much more moderate in its voices and views during Birdsall's tenure.

The early feminist magazines have been seen mainly in terms of their interplay with the "masculine" mainstream press of the day. Most emphasize what Ann Russo and Cheris Kramarae do, that the feminist magazines "publicized a broad range of women's issues and protests at a time when many men editors throughout the country were transmitting messages hostile to women's rights."[7] The oppositional status they register—where feminist magazines foster critical response to man-made images of women—is vital to understanding much of what the early feminist press attempted and accomplished. Yet it remains only part of the story.

The first American feminist magazines also organized effective "internal" protests, engaging in critical dialogue with dominant—and to some extent woman-authored—gender discourse. By this time, there was plenty to fight on many fronts. The feminist magazines emerged amidst the so-called feminine fifties, when the popularity of the sentimental-domestic novel was beginning to peak and commercial ladies' magazines were likewise attaining substantial public notice and profitability. The best-selling women's magazines of the nineteenth century—including *Godey's Lady's Book* (1830–98) published by Louis Godey; the *Peterson Magazine* (1842–98) published by the writer C.J. Peterson; and *Arthur's (Home) Magazine* (1852–98) published by popular novelist T.S. Arthur—boasted circulations of 40,000 by the time the *Lily* appeared, and grew to more than 150,000 through the antebellum era.[8] Although these popular magazines were male dominated on the business side, a growing breed of literary women, perhaps most notably Sarah Hale, visibly and vocally ran the editorial side.[9]

At its height in 1855, the *Lily* achieved circulation of about 6,000 subscribers nationwide—half the circulation of 12,000 averaged by all women's monthlies at mid-century, and nearly equal to the average circulation of all American monthly magazines at the time.[10] Although the magazine survived mostly by subscription instead of advertising,[11] the significance of the *Lily* did not lie in its numbers, but in its dynamic operations.

The *Lily* and her sisters were the hosts of repeated confrontations with the gender discourse popularized by the mainstream women's magazines of the day—with claims of woman's innate moral purity, virtue, and "influence";[12] with the corresponding vision of social organization, "the woman's sphere;" and with the formula of the sentimental-domestic or "woman's" novel. Issue after issue, month after month, such dominant gender discourse was deployed in various formats and debated in the various departments of the feminist magazines. This process of persistent articulation and reflection, repetition and recycling—hallmarks of the American magazine format since its inception—promoted discursive innovation and revision over time. Other formal qualities of the magazine, its rhythm of periodical publication, serial style of contribution and reception, and episodic reading, further supported these outcomes. Finally, some conditions of the periodical industry of the day, such as the practice of clipping copy, also assisted in promoting transformation. Taken together, the formal dynamics, discursive practices, and periodical pressures at play in the early American feminist magazines enabled women to challenge the boundaries of popularized "femininity," pushing it into new realms of female empowerment.

DISCURSIVE DEPLOYMENTS: USING SENTIMENTAL-DOMESTICITY STRATEGICALLY

Early feminist editors emphasized the distinction between feminist "women" and sentimental-domestic "ladies."[13] Nevertheless, sentimental styles and several of its definitive tropes frequently appeared in the pages of the *Lily* and her sisters.[14]

That makes historical and rhetorical sense. The first-generation feminist magazines were largely written and read by the same cohort of white, middle-class women who, along with their relatives, neighbors, and other demographic kin, were making the "woman's novel" and women's magazines so successful in the literary marketplace. Contributors to feminist magazines were steeped in that language, both as readers and as gendered speakers in their daily lives.

Such intimate experience enabled the more savvy to exploit the popular discourse for their own purposes. In the feminist magazines, numerous contributors capitalized on what was the central selling point of the sentimental mode: its capacity to arouse emotional engagement. After all, the sentimental voice almost literally cries out for reader response. *Lily* writers developed ways to rally that response to the cause of social change.

One early example of this strategic use of the sentimental was contributed by Mary C. Vaughan, a president of the New York State Temperance Society and later the editor of the *Woman's Temperance Paper* (1854–56).[15] Vaughan herself experienced a conversion through her long-term involvement with the *Lily*. Over a two-year period of regular contribution, she was transformed from a firm believer in the gendered doctrine of separate spheres (December 1850) to a commitment to dress reform (June 1851), women's education (October 1852), property rights (October 1852), and even divorce (October 1851) and suffrage (November 1851).[16]

Vaughan's February 1851 article, "Maternal Influence," appeared just on the cusp of this change of heart. She begins with a question at the very core of sentimental domesticity: "a mother's influence—who can estimate its strength or its power?"

At the outset, Vaughan's answer is more poetic than political: "None can limit its extent, for whether for good or evil, it shall be felt through the ceaseless ages of eternity." In a style so heightened as to be syntactically dizzying, Vaughan then expounds that "none may know in this life of the souls encouraged by maternal solicitude to heavenward aspirations; fitted by maternal prayers and examples, when death has dissolved the ties that bound them to earthly influences, to plume their flight beyond the stars, and join evermore in the grand employments of the better world." In the same sentence, conjoined merely by the conjunction "and," Vaughan's opening paragraph then plummets downward, warning: "and the wailings of the lost through all their long eternity of woe, will add a deeper torment to the faithless mother's doom."

The pain, of course, begins long before eternity. "This bitter punishment commences even in this life," she admonishes, "where there is no joy but the consciousness of duties well fulfilled . . . the faithful mother, whose prayers and counsels have guided the feet of her child in the straight and narrow path, has peace and great joy, alas!" Vaughan plunges again, this time with only a comma separating bliss from the onset of degradation and death. "How bitter is the condemnation of her who has failed to warn the child her Maker gave to be trained for heaven, when temptation beckoned him into the alluring paths of sin; when she sees the soul which came to her pure and unsullied, all written over with the black characters of moral pollution and death."[17]

Vaughan's highly emotionalized rhetoric, her spiraling structure, and her commingling of maternal success with heavenly rewards (and maternal failure with hellish punition) captures the cosmic dimensions and stirring style of the sentimental-domestic voice. At the center of this whirlwind is, of course, the figure of The Mother. If "faithful" to the "vast responsibility" of motherhood, Vaughan's rhetoric links maternity to eternal bliss; however, if a "failed" mother, Vaughan's rhetoric plummets precipitously, from beauteous childbirth to blackness and death.

Vaughan, a writer and future editor, was a rising expert in sentimental-domestic rhetoric. She was able to exploit this language, deploying it tactically for a single (if lengthy) paragraph, only to shift abruptly to more pragmatic prose in the next one.

"This train of thought was induced," she announces, "by hearing of the illness in the prison of our city of one whom I knew in other days and very different circumstances." "Sometime since," she reports, "while under the influence of ardent spirits, he committed theft and was arrested and imprisoned."

Vaughan then writes the story of a drunkard's decline. As she shifts to narrate it, she exposes the pragmatic utility of sentimentality for rousing readers. The kind of stirring rhetoric she deploys, readers are both told and shown, is a state of mind that one achieves, or is moved to, under certain kinds of compelling circumstances. Vaughan apparently realized that, by 1851, this was a discourse powerful enough with her readers to move them to the agitated state her cause, temperance activism, would require to hold sway.

Vaughan is developing a discursive concoction, one ready and able to promote emerging activist ends. In the final paragraph, she takes her last, best shot at getting readers to rise up and join a fight for change. To close, Vaughan re-enhances her language again, although hardly returning to the heights and lengths to which she had gone before. She keeps grounded this time by speaking as an author rather than a narrator, and by keeping her sights fixed on the readers she hopes to have close by her side. "Oh! that mothers would take warning by such fatal examples," she writes. "That they would ever remember the vast responsibility which rests upon them as they write upon the unsullied soul the characters that shall stand there at the Judgment Day, to determine the weal or woe of the beloved ones entrusted to their care."

Vaughan deploys spiraling sentimental-domestic rhetoric to rouse women readers, then tells a tale of woe, and finally ends with a suggestive authorial entreaty to her readers. Structurally, this piece presages an important format for the feminist magazines—especially in that closing. Although oblique in this early form, Vaughan's concluding device, distinct in its rhetoric and in its audience awareness, is a kind of "authorial addendum." It is a space in which the writer implies, gestures toward, or directly calls for action based on the social conditions her narrative has revealed.

Vaughan was an early practitioner of the authorial addendum, but she was not the only writer to wield it. In fact, numerous writers, professional and amateur alike, soon grasped the virtue of tacking on an authorial addendum to a sentimentalized story, thus giving themselves a distinct space for prodding women readers toward action based on the emotional response roused by material they had read.[18]

These early feminist writers probably came by the device through its history in moral reform journalism of the 1820s and '30s.[19] There, similar scenarios, where woman-centered stories are attached with sermonlike riders, can sometimes be found. An 1836 serial published in the *Advocate of Moral Reform* (1835–41), for example, is an exposé in a sentimental-domestic mode.[20] The serial describes in domestic-novel detail the agonizing story of an innocent young woman, seduced with the promise of marriage, who is instead drugged, deflowered, and left to die in childbirth by her intended.[21] This sentimental melodrama is attached with the author's explicit warning to women readers about real life. In this case, the writer tells readers to take action to protect themselves against the excesses of men, even those who appear to be respectable gentlemen.

Given its early history in such Protestant-leaning women's reform writing, it is not surprising to find the authorial addendum cropping up first in temperance pieces such as Vaughan's. After all, the temperance tale is a child of the moral reform narrative as well as a relative of the sentimental-domestic novel. All share a common cause in the thematic dedication to the security of women and children. And plotlines typically portray good women and innocent children punished by the poverty, misery, and fear that result from the excesses of men on whom they are dependent. All of these story types could yield feminist conclusions—depending on how they were read.[22] Little wonder, then, that the authorial addendum was so often used to prod, guide, or escort readers in feminist directions.

After temperance, what Mary Ryan has named the "cult of the mother" is the next most common topic to be politicized by use of the authorial addendum.[23] A February 1854 *Lily* contribution is suggestively titled "Woman's Influence and Duty." The author begins on a standard sentimental-domestic note: "Woman's influence is great and universal," she agrees. Although men are unwilling to acknowledge the "great and unmeasured influence of women in regulating the more important affairs of life," she continues, her rhetoric mounting to sentimental-domestic heights, "still it is felt;—felt from the time [the little baby] prattles at his mother's knees, till in all his dignity he walks forth a man; and hence the adage," she concludes, now embracing the sentimental-domestic tradition by use of its unofficial motto, "they that rock the cradle, rule the world."

Her addendum then addresses this power directly—and directly to her audience. "Mothers, and wives of this vast republic!" she hails. "Although we are not permitted to occupy the Presidential chair, or sit in our halls of legislation, still we have voices which will reach where the statesman and orator cannot be heard. . . . For "let it be remembered," she warns, perhaps speaking to the wider reading-public, "that from the hearthstone of every citizen issue forth the errors and prejudices which govern the world."

Women's employment followed. Ann McDowell's *Woman's Advocate*, which focused on the politics of women's labor, is rife with examples. A January 1856 contribution calls on sentimentality to start, asking "sympathizing souls" who can see "the hallowing influence of a mother's love and holy precept" to understand why women must work for wages. She then turns to sentimentalized pity, asking "kind hearts that pity, generous souls that thrill with indignation at the recital of [women's] wrongs, and the starvation prices allotted to them," to further rouse emotional support.

Then, her authorial addendum speaks right to readers in a very different voice. "O! noble daughters of labor," she calls out, ". . . let your own voices be raised in just resentment of further impositions. *Demand* the equal rights of labor; the rights of liberty; the equality that mind, heart, and spirit give."

As the authorial addendum came into wider and more frequent use in the feminist magazines, it became a recognizable reformist formula. To remain effective, therefore, it had to change. New angles were needed to maintain the engagement necessary for the structuring strategy to work.

To refresh effectiveness, many contributors intensified narrative intimacy, whether they had personal knowledge of the characters and events described or not. A February 1852 *Lily* contribution relates the tale of the "unhappy wife of a drunkard" third-hand. The contributor had read about the woman in a publication from a group called the Carson Society, which itself had cribbed the case from a piece in the New York *Daily Times*.[24] Even so, the authorial addendum calls out with immediacy and a strong sense of personal connection:

Oh woman! Be not deceived with idle words! Believe not that you are a weak, irresponsible being, and that it is for you to rest solely upon a man's strength and submit unmurmuringly to the fate he brings upon you! Oh! Woman! If you have a spark of life in your soul, if you have a feeling of mercy towards your sex, if you have the pride which belongs to a noble spirit in your heart, arouse from the lethargy which has fallen upon you and gird yourself for the deliverance of your suffering and oppressed sisters, from the hands of cruel men!

A second strategy was to shoot straighter at the goal of activism. As late as January 1863, a *Sibyl* contributor was still using an authorial addendum—and in it she doesn't pull any punches about what she wants readers to do. The writer, Louisa T. Whittier, uses the sentimental structure to recite woman's trials:

just as long as woman is, for the want of a home and the necessaries of life, forced to 'promise to obey' a man she does not love, and who is entirely unadapted to her nature . . . while woman is by law and public opinion denied legal rights and privileges with man—shut out from many of the most lucrative employments, and but half paid for what she is allowed to do, so long will 'marrying for a home' be the legitimate result.

Whittier's authorial addendum directly advocates action on the issue of married women's independence: "Women of America, it is to you that I make an appeal to rouse yourself to action; throw off the fetters which a false public opinion has fastened upon you; . . . make yourselves worthy of a higher position in life than the darling, angel, pet, slave of any human being."

In all its permutations, the structural device of the authorial addendum signaled as it simultaneously created a formal space for links between popular literature and life, between media and reality. It served two important needs. First, it allowed middle-class women to speak critically and politically without compromising their considerable, accepted eloquence and authority as "ladies." And, it helped middle-class women of various stripes connect through shared emotion and familiar language. Since the addendum merely brought forward the latent implications of popular narratives, the authors who used it could be seen as honest uniters, not traitors to traditional womanhood; they could rally reading women while maintaining the integrity of both the popular voice and their politics. The device thereby helped women writers move from the popular to the political—and to bring the considerable clout and demonstrated commitment of middle-class reading women with them.

The grand optimism of this organizing power is captured in a variation of the authorial addendum, which appeared in the *Lily*'s August 1856 issue. (The piece was reprinted from a sister feminist periodical, McDowell's *Woman's Advocate*.) Written by Elizabeth Oakes Smith, a contributor to the *Lily* as well as to numerous popular women's magazines,[25] the piece attests to the by-now-established efficacy of the device.

Oakes Smith wants to make what was, in 1856, an unheard-of, revolutionary call: for suffrage. She begins matter-of-factly, with practical, observable fact and fait accompli. Women are "already bearing the burdens of citizenship," she says. By "toil and poverty," and by "taxation, responsibility and labor," she explains, women "are forced into the forefront of the battle in the hard contest for bread, and are exposed to all the temptations and hazards which our brothers so feelingly enumerate as threatening to us."

Like so many before her, Oakes Smith concludes with an authorial addendum. But she uses its rhetorical difference and distinctive purpose in a novel way. Rather than attaching a political rider to a sentimental-domestic tale of womanly woe or weal, she reverses the typical organization, appending a sentimental-domestic promise of eternal perfection to a contribution that had recited immediate social conditions as arguments for unprecedented political change. Oakes Smith uses the authorial addendum to promise her audience that heaven on earth is but a vote and a hyphen away: "Do away with this glaring inconsistency, and women have little more to ask—the eternal harmonies will roll on, human governments represent better human justice and divine love, and this senseless cry of 'out of her sphere' be as little applicable to woman as to the planet which, morning or evening, lends its clear beautiful beams to gild the early or later day."[26]

REPETITION AND REVISIONISM: PERIODICAL PRESSURES AND THE "WOMAN'S SPHERE"

The sentimental-domestic deployments by Vaughan, Oakes Smith, and others are "writerly" tactics supported by the *Lily*'s politics and pages. But wider industry conventions, and the periodical qualities of the magazine form itself, also enhanced the *Lily*'s potential to promote change.

Take the common industry practice of pirating copy. In America, the publication of pilfered copy had a long political history. In the 1740s, as we have seen, the concept of "press liberty" was in part developed through pirating.[27] Arguments for the American Revolution were similarly evolved and spread by pirating in the 1770s.[28]

In the *Lily*, copy was pulled from literary magazines, newspapers, commercial women's magazines, some farm and trade publications, books (particularly collections of essays of short stories), and also other feminist or reform periodicals. Accordingly, reprinted articles were written by a range of writers, from very conservative sentimental-domestic authors, such as Mrs. Lydia Sigourney (in February 1850; January 1851; February 1855); to more politically centrist woman novelists, such as Virginia Townsend (September 1855); to more radical or renowned women of the popular press, including Harriet Beecher Stowe (October 1850), Jane Grey Swisshelm (August 1851; December 1854), Fanny Fern, and Grace Greenwood (whose feminist magazine articles, both pirated and original, are too numerous to list). Since the *Lily* pirated by theme or sentiment rather than the star power that was beginning to touch the industry at this time, amateur and anonymous contributions shared pages with published authors and movement leaders. Although individual *Lily* issues varied in their use of recycled copy—some numbers contain almost exclusively original material, whereas others present 25 percent reprinted content—overall, this industry practice was well in evidence in all the first-generation feminist magazines.

Pilfered copy helped the *Lily* and her sister magazines get into the thick of things. It allowed small-circulating, politically marginal, out-of-town periodicals to participate in the influential world of the nationalizing popular press. It let them bring in big-league news and feature copy, and deal with it on editorially equal terms. Pirating also enhanced the polyvocality and breadth of the magazines' coverage. And it enabled the feminist magazines to champion certain chosen ideas or positions, perpetuating their public lives in print.

Clipping copy also helped augment the feminist magazines' communities of readers. Patricia Okker has written that nineteenth-century women's magazines developed and deployed a "sisterly editorial voice" that, "with its gendered basis of authority and informal exchange between readers and editors, often affected not only the tone of the editorial columns but the very form of the periodical as well."[29] Linda Steiner has also noted the self-conscious sisterhood construed within women's periodicals around this time, arguing, although too narrowly, that this idea was distinctive to the women's suffrage press.[30] It wasn't; as we have seen, mainstream women's magazines fostered and circulated ideas about their own sisterly community since their very inception in the late eighteenth century.[31] (Indeed, even today's women's magazines still evoke or actively deploy this sisterly self-image.) Clipped copy enhanced this image, suggesting momentum and an ever-widening "sisterhood." It implied that everybody was talking about women's rights—a belief that could then become a self-fulfilling prophecy.

The idea of "sisterhood" is telegraphed in an April 1850 article pirated from Jane Grey Swisshelm's *Pittsburgh Saturday Visiter* (1848–57).[32] Written by a professional journalist and feminist, Frances Dana Gage,[33] it takes up a topic near and dear to the heart of literary womanhood in the 1850s: the so-called "woman's sphere."

To gainsay the predominant separate spheres model of the world, Gage calls upon a literal form of sisterhood: her own matriarchal family line. She envisions her grandmother, "a small, delicate woman . . . , the mother of seven or eight carrying on horseback a two-year-old baby, . . . [who] toil[ed] slowly but wearily by the precipitous and dangerous paths to the heights of the Alleghanies." Then, she describes her mother, "*a Dana*— just as likely as not one of the eloquent lecturer's own born relations, . . . trudging by her side on foot, stick in hand, urging along the old cow." With these homey, all-American examples, the writer directly contradicts male-authored myths of female frailty that the "woman's sphere" responds to and reinscribes. "It was all the men were able to do to help along the ox teams" during this trek to the Western frontier, she jibes.

Having situated her argument in the context of personal history, she is then in a position to authoritatively ask, "Were they in there [*sic*] 'sphere'? by the 'fireside'? 'softening themselves for man's bolder look'?" "Were they taking upon themselves 'duties assigned to them'? Or were they only trying to be 'mannish'?" she presses. Forcing the two dominant male-authored characterizations of women—"feminine" frailty and "feminist" mannishness—into direct contact with each other, the writer suggests that both are foolish fictions, inconsistent with the realities of women's experiences and responses in American history.

Gage's article was pirated in part to add its arguments to a larger critical assault taking place in all the feminist magazines: a battle against the prevailing concept of the "woman's sphere." Indeed, the vision of a sex-segregated world this space signified was a thematic obsession in the magazines. Treatments of this topic, both pirated and original, in both prose and poetry (e.g., February 15, 1854), by both amateurs and professionals, persistently appeared. The repeated treatment of the "woman's sphere"—

item after item, page after page, month after month, year upon year—organized varied contributions into a progressive, serial assault team, and various contributors into an effective, collective fighting force.

"The Appropriate Sphere of Woman," a June 1851 contribution to the *Lily*, uses spatial metaphors to combat limitations. Rhetorically, it works to renovate "woman's sphere" as if it were an outgrown room or home. "Man, in his generosity," the contributor begins sarcastically, "has carefully and repeatedly measured its length and breadth and drawn its boundaries, . . . and woman," she continues, "has . . . studiously curbed her thoughts and actions, lest they should be found protruding."

In consequence of such prescribed restriction, the writer explains, "young women generally have not engaged in pursuits which would give full scope to all their faculties and energies." The liberty the writer wants, she quickly asserts, would better "fit [women] to truly perform the sacred duties of wife and mother, as well as render them independent of the contingency of marriage for sources of activity and the means of a livelihood." Here is another example of the use of domestic discourse to build toward women's empowerment. The "woman's sphere" that is meant to enshrine maternal capacities actually restricts and even debases it. The contribution pushes on domestic discourse from within its own boundaries, asserting that women will make bad mothers "as well as" dependent and miserable individuals if her "appropriate" sphere is not expanded. This particular strategy, an important one, will be addressed shortly.

"Woman's Sphere—What Is It?" (July 1854) makes a narrative out of this drift, in effect marching woman out of the delimited space on her own track record. Beginning with the recent past available to her personal recollection, the writer notes, "I have to refer back but a short period of time, to find women excluded from the privileges of education; and when one dared brave public opinion and claim that privilege, you very well know the result. The same cry was raised that we hear now when a woman dares to step out of her prescribed circle—'Out of Her Sphere!'" However, "it was discovered that woman could be educated without delicacy and refinement sustaining any serious injury; therefore she has been allowed *some* of the privileges of education—not all—. . . thus was her sphere widened."

Working from education to women's writing, from self-knowledge to self-representation, the same logic applies: "it was found that she was capable of writing; and after the stigma attached to the appellation of 'literary women' was removed, female authors appeared before the world, who well compared with authors of the other sex." Indeed, in marketplace terms, many of these women writers surpassed their male colleagues. And women's magazines, such as Hale's and others, played a vital role in making the "appellation of 'literary women'" consistent with certain notions of "femininity" now at play in the feminist magazines.[34]

Moving into the present moment, the contributor's tone becomes more challenging and her language more legalistic. She is pushing to the next step: "Many assert that woman is not man's equal in strength of mind. I say to all such—let them prove it. Has her strength of mind not proved sufficient to accomplishment of all she has yet undertaken?" To this the contributor quickly answers, then questions again: "Most assuredly it has; and who dare make the assertion that she is not competent to perform all she shall hereafter undertake?" The contributor's rhetorical questions capitalize on a version of women's history purveyed in and by the magazine. And it doubly dares. The writer simultaneously uses the collaborative capacities of the *Lily* to challenge women to collectively assert their competence, and the oppositional mode of the magazine to defy a wider, public audience to deny women's demonstrated progress.

By the time an April 1855 letter-to-the-editor of the *Lily* is contributed, the writer, "Martha," can dislodge the cultural notion of "woman's sphere" at the outset. The contribution takes as a premise that woman's "place" ought to be a matter of her personal choice, seriously problematizing the notion of a culturally prescribed place for women at all. "Much at the present time is said of 'woman's wishing to get out of her proper place.' Now where shall we locate this much talked of place?" she coyly inquires. Then she asks more pointedly, "Shall man, or God, or woman herself be permitted to choose?"

Having quickly asserted a woman's right to choose her appropriate place in the world, Martha can transcend the boundaries of the "woman's sphere"—or, at least, make dimensions a moot point by extending boundaries to the very ends of the earth. Like Oakes Smith and some other contributors both before her, Martha here conjoins with hyphens, mere dashes of her pen, women's immediate, secular, and legal status with promises of ultimate, cosmic and abstract outcomes:

Women who will boldly assert themselves as responsible *individuals,* claim rights which the good time coming will assuredly grant— the good time when the words "sex" and "color" will as universally be stricken from our statutes, as that those laws are now rendered more voluminous by the frequent repetition of "white male citizen"—when the boundaries of woman's sphere will be the boundaries of heaven and earth.

Martha explodes the "woman's sphere"—indeed also the racial exclusion and hierarchy that it perpetrates—and replaces it with a vision of heaven on earth composed of liberty and justice for all. In this truly more-perfect union, Martha concludes, "there is no circumscribed sphere."

Frances Gage again takes up the topic, this time in an original piece written for the *Lily*. She picks up where Martha has left off. Gage blithely dismisses the whole notion of a "woman's sphere" at the outset. For her, the sphere need not be argumentatively displaced; it has already been quite casually misplaced. "Girls, I will tell you the plain truth. If ever I had a sphere—a sphere peculiar to a woman—fashioned after the models of the present age, I must have lost it a great many years ago," she writes. After recounting incidents from her lived experience in which she acted independently, she concludes that, "then, instead of shrinking myself within it, I took my station outside it, to travel whenever I pleased in its pleasant paths."

Gage looks back only long enough to affirm that domestic discourse has laid the foundation for her feminist politics: "let me tell you," she assures her sisters, "I have found my home sphere—just the thing for a wife and mother—and on its wide spread, elevated, beautiful and harmonious surface I have built my platform of Woman's Rights, and on that platform I intend to stand fearless and free while I stand at all." She will have liberty or death, she suggests. In closing, she vows, "I shall advocate with earnestness and doctrine, that all the energies that God gave woman should be used in the very best advantage,"—and here the progression from "home sphere" to "woman's rights" is clearly figured—"for herself, for her family, and for society."

Such treatments of the "woman's sphere," coming from various angles and points of view, relentlessly assaulted the concept until it was eroded, exploded, or simply left behind in the dust. And the effect of these various contributions was enhanced by the magazine's periodical rhythm of publication. Monthly repetition lent articles an inescapable, cumulative effect: together, from month to month to month, they made serious inroads in the "woman's sphere," finally accomplishing its undoing.

Other periodical qualities also helped. "Woman's Sphere," a series written as an original "for the *Lily*," reveals another aspect of the periodical qualities at play. The series, submitted by a contributor perhaps pseudonymously called "Belle Ville" (or "beautiful city" in French), wants to march women out of her prescribed sphere. In that effort, the writer reaches for arguments that are somewhat beyond her grasp. Yet the episodic structure of periodical publication helps her across logical lapses, allowing her to advance toward increasingly progressive claims, and with her readers in tow.

Ville's first "Woman's Sphere" article appears in the *Lily*'s September 15, 1854, issue. She begins on well-trodden ground to argue that woman's innate moral sense naturally qualifies her for the pulpit. "When [woman] attempts to teach the principles of morality . . . then the cry is heard echoing long and loud, 'woman's sphere,' and we are told that 'she is out of her place.'" "Why, I ask, is she out of her place?" Ville wonders. "Is she not competent to fill that exalted station?"[35]

Addressing this concern, she deploys the fundamental equality of Christian souls argument, a line of reasoning by then a staple in antebellum reform writing owing to its extensive use in abolitionism.[36] Woman was "endowed from the beginning with the same moral, intellectual and physical faculties as man—placed side by side with him in the Garden of Eden—empowered to exercise equal authority or dominion with him over the beasts of the field &c," Ville writes, so "she could not have been otherwise than equal to him."

"Yet," she turns, pitting Christian dogma against cultural construction, "how many are there at the present day who strenuously contend that 'man is born to rule, and woman to 'obey'"—"that 'man is the *lord* of creation'—and consequently that to him, with all reverence and fear, must woman bow in humble submission." These claims, Ville writes, "are but mere assertions," which don't stand up to either analysis or experience. "When reasons are called for to sustain such assertions," she presses, "none can be given."

Ville proceeds, summoning by turns nature, God, and lived experience, the three discourses intimately familiar to her through their use in gender construction (in the case of God and nature) and in early American women's magazine writing (in the case of experience): "You may search the entire contents of the wide and extensive book of Nature—turn from these to the volume of the Divine revelation and fathom the utmost depths of common sense and no such reasons can be found." Her idiom may be uneven, but she does manage to get her point across: "With the records of the past—the view of the present all open before our gaze, we are led to the conclusion that morality is, and always has been, found in the greatest extent among the female portion of the community."

Emboldened by past success, Ville's next entry, November 15, 1854, ventures onto newer ground. "Having in a previous number briefly . . . shown that [woman] is not out of her sphere when she undertakes to proclaim from the pulpit the glad tidings of salvation," she asserts, "we come in the next place to contrast their mental capabilities and powers, and thereby show that the whole field of intellectual labor is open to her, and that she is not out of her sphere in laboring therein." "It follows, then, as a necessary consequence," she contends, "that if the same amount of cultivation be expended upon each, their development will be equal."[37]

Ville then tries to cover the whole complicated case against unequal access to education and "cultivation": "The cultivation of the mental faculties improves them; therefore, that sex upon whom the greatest amount of cultivation is expended, will be considered as superior in intellectual attainment or capacity; and hence exists the erroneous impression within the minds of many who are not able to, or at least do not, distinguish between natural and acquired powers, and therefore conclude that the female sex is inferior in point of mental capacity," she argues.

Ville, too, has difficulty distinguishing effectively between "capacity" and "attainment." However, her logical lapses are bridged by the *Lily*'s periodical publication. The magazine routinely skims across gaps in contributors' thinking, vitiating breaches with every new issue to come off the press. And among readers, such inconsistencies or complications may be forgotten in interim periods, resolved by subsequent contributors, or bridged in their own ways. Meanwhile, Ville can move on, claiming in her December 1854 entry that "having thus briefly shown that the female sex are not inferior to the male in their mental organization," she will now proceed to provide women with full and active participation in the American public. She promises "to show that they would not be out of their sphere in exercising those powers which have been given unto them by an All-wise Creator for some purpose other than to lie dormant and inactive; as in a majority of cases they have been, and still are, suffered to do."[38] Ville's next entry, a letter published in the March 15, 1855, issue, moves full steam ahead, confident that all previous points are secure.

FORMATTING FOR FEMINISM: REFASHIONING POPULAR FORMULAS

The various dynamics at play on the level of popular discourse in the *Lily* also operated on popular literary genres, on the level of formula. The magazine helped create new kinds of creative writers and critical readers, women charged to rethink the popular stories underwriting imaginative possibilities for women's lives.

At the time when the *Lily* and her sister appeared, the sentimental-domestic or "woman's" novel was in its popular heyday. Readers and reviewers alike, as Nina Baym has shown, recognized the distinctive style and tradition of these novels; it had become formula fiction.[39]

Contemporary critics of women's popular culture still debate about whether these woman-authored, woman-centered stories offered empowering or entrapping messages to audiences. But answers to these questions depend now, as they depended in 1850, on individual cultural spin and individual insight, on how writers and readers saw them.

Amelia Bloomer, the *Lily's* editor, was both.[40] In a letter sequence exchanged with T.S. Arthur, the popular novelist and editor of the weekly *Arthur's Home Gazette* (1850–54), soon to be absorbed into *Arthur's (Home) Magazine* (1852–98), she dons both hats to bring new meaning to Arthur's new sentimental-domestic novel, *Ruling a Wife* (1850).[41]

Like the sentimental-domestic novel, the letter, too, was a strongly gendered genre of writing. And it remained resonant for women writers, and particularly within the women's magazine tradition, through the time when the Bloomer-Arthur letters appeared.[42] Like Eliza in her response to her seducer, and many women's magazine contributors since, Bloomer uses the form and functions of the letter to mount a crucial critique of male mistreatment and constitute a woman's point of view.

Sentimental-domestic novels such as Arthur's are tales of social relations with a heroine at the heart. Typically, they detail the trials and triumph of this female protagonist who has been orphaned, and who is egregiously mistreated by the very authorities in her life who ought to have nurtured and protected her. The heroine's virtuous character is often demonstrated and measured against a double, another but lesser woman, who is seen to be seduced by luxury or status, for example, or who is conniving, duplicitous, or even vicious—who is somehow fallen in distinctly gendered ways. Plotlines recount the heroine's achievement of identity, of autonomy and self-respect, despite the inequitable treatment and cultural obstacles repeatedly thrown up in her way. Neither her tragic personal circumstances, nor the violent treatment to which she is sometimes subjected, nor the debilitating limitations placed on her sex prevents the female protagonist of the sentimental-domestic novel from becoming a literary heroine in both gendered and American terms: by the repeated exercise of her virtuous character, she achieves self-reliance.

But Arthur's rendering of the formula had subverted this potentially empowering message, so Bloomer's letter is a pronounced rebuke. She opens with "an abstract" of the novel that appropriates this sentimental-domestic plotline to critique Arthur's use of it. "Mr. Lane, the hero of the story," she writes, "was an overbearing, lordly husband, who looked upon his wife as in every respect his inferior, and from whom he extracted the most perfect submission." As is too often the case with absolute power, Lane's "desire to rule increased with time," she continues, "and time also opened her eyes more clearly to a sense of her abject slavery." Mrs. Lane's consciousness is fully raised when her maternal authority—the ideological center of domesticity—is contravened by her husband: a "child was given to them . . . and the father made it his business to direct in the nursery, and to order this and that treatment for the child, contrary to the better judgment of the mother." At this violation of Mrs. Lane's only accredited authority, "her dormant spirit was at length aroused."

This damage to the foundation of the domestic novel causes that narrative to collapse. Mrs. Lane, "with her baby," fled "to the city," where, swindled of her "last dollar," she finds herself alone, destitute and desperate. "A man passing" overhears her description of her plight to another woman, a trope that has referred to women's public powerlessness since the rise of the women's magazine genre. He offers "to take Mrs. L. under his protection," and "to escort her . . . to the United States Hotel." Unfortunately, the con man and his painted helpmate connive to "deceive her," instead conveying her "to a house of prostitution!"[43] Mrs. Lane "attempted to leave the house," but "escape was impossible—she was locked in!" Although she wields the supposedly powerful instrument of "female influence" by making "the most heart-touching appeals" for sympathy, "all [were] in vain," Bloomer recounts.

Bloomer's frustration with Arthur's story peaks as she reaches his climax. "While they were dragging [Mrs. Lane] from the room—she in the meanwhile wringing her hands and shrieking for mercy—the door was open," Bloomer relates, and who but "Mr. Lane stood before them!". "This," Bloomer dashes, "is the substance of the story." Unable to let it stand unanswered even for a moment, she proceeds, lodging "our objections" to the story in the same paragraph.

Nobody asks what on earth Mr. Lane is doing visiting a brothel. Evidently, Bloomer's questions are oriented elsewhere, and are remarkably similar to those raised and written by contemporary feminist critics who reveal the debilitating implications embedded, along with more empowering ones, in the sentimental-domestic story. The *Lily* reviewer can barely contain her critique. Her outrage burns all the way down to her grammar: one paragraph—long on commas and furious dashes and short on the more calming and placid periods—lists her grievances. "You have only shown that we are weak and helpless—incapable of taking care of ourselves or keeping out of harm's way," she charges. She summons the sentimental structure through recitation of the heroine's trials by Arthur's hand: "No matter to how bad a man a woman is tied—no matter to how much insult she may be subjected—no matter . . . her feelings, and . . . the indifference and scorn [of] her opinions, no matter how he won her young heart with promises of . . . love [only to] be transformed into a demon—and her disgust and loathing"—Bloomer barely stops to breathe—"you have shown us that it is useless for a woman to think of freeing herself . . . [for] . . . should she attempt, she will fall into the snares and dangers from which she is powerless to extricate herself, and which will speedily cause her to repent the step and sigh and return." "But," Bloomer rails, to the very marriage "from which there is no escape, and this same cruel man from whom she has fled comes to her rescue."

"Now, Mr. Arthur," she reproves, taking the author to task, "I believe . . . that any woman high-souled enough to take the step which Mrs. Lane did, would be capable of taking care of herself and keeping her character unspotted." "I believe, sir," she continues, that "there are thousands of wronged and degraded women, who, if they would throw off the yoke that binds them, would show to the world that it was only while enslaved that they were incapable of self protection." Rhetorically liberating women from the confines of Arthur's (indeed, society's) snare, Bloomer imagines a truly heroic heroine at the center of a new rendering of the story: "[W]hen freed," she continues, women "could provide for themselves, meet dangers, resist temptations, bid defiance to the libertine, or, if insulted, revenge the insult."

Bloomer wants and demands this different story. "Why did you not," she questions, challenging Arthur's use of the woman's novel for male purposes, "let Mrs. Lane show that she was equal to the emergency in which you placed her?" Pushing the boundaries of the sentimental story line to its limits, she asks further, "Why not let her rise superior to so dependent and so *degrading* a position?" Advancing on, she demands still more: "Why not let her seek and find some honorable employment, where, if but for a day, she might support herself and her child by her own independent exertions?"

Bloomer's repeated challenges mount a substantive critique of the sentimental story, at least when put to male use. She charges that Arthur's "design was to teach woman that she is inferior and that it is her duty to yield in all cases to her self-constituted lord and master, even though she be . . . brutalized." "Instead of elevating the character of women, and teaching her to respect herself"—an empowering possibility of the domestic story—"you have humbled her in her own eyes, and those of the world." His choosing to debilitate women, Bloomer suggests, has "caused her to blush with shame and indignation, that man's companion and equal," a radical image at this time, "should be seen so weak and dependent," a retrograde one.

Middle-class women readers in 1850 would have quickly grasped that such deep defilement of a lady compels corrective action. A second letter from Bloomer to Arthur follows in the November 1850 issue. Calmer with time, she explains: "I think women should exercise great forbearance, and put up with many things hard to endure before resorting to the extreme step of separation," Bloomer writes. "Yet," she delimits, "I believe there is a point beyond which endurance ceases to be a virtue." Beyond that point, she explains, "it is both her right and her duty to seek safety and peace."

A critical ideological transition is written here, precisely using prevailing gender ideology to make the turn. By conjoining "rights" and "duties" together under the rubric of woman's "virtue," Bloomer uses popular notions of women's identity to pivot toward her more-radical hopes for female emancipation. Bloomer both delimits and expands—she critically redefines—the strongly gendered notion of "feminine virtue." In her reconstruction, there is a point beyond which the seemingly endless of requirements of virtue cannot go without discrediting that very discourse. At that moment—the moment when virtue may be undone—a good woman is obliged to act. It becomes her duty, an accredited "feminine" response, as well as her "right," a new feminist endowment, to act independently, and in the interest of herself. Here the popular gender discourse is challenged from within itself, so it demands, by its own dictates, a new (yet still accredited) response. The popular discourse of "feminine virtue" has been transformed so as to reach—indeed require—the autonomy, self-sufficiency, and strength this idea had previously effaced or opposed.

This kind of turn—accomplished by pushing domestic discourse to its own extremes, so that one element confounds or contradicts other, definitive elements, threatening to explode the whole configuration—presages the 1851 claim in "The Appropriate Sphere of Woman" that this space must be widened lest it debilitate the very maternal nurture it purports to promote. It also prefigures Elizabeth Oakes Smith's 1854 use of woman's supposed moral purity and exemplarity to demand her involvement in the dirty, public electoral process. This strategy, a kind of discursive pressure politics, in which the various strands of popular gender discourse are pushed into confounding contact with one another, was so common in the first-generation feminist magazines that it continued in many forms of women's reform writing through the nineteenth century. It is put to use in justifications for the "social purity" movement, in the renewed temperance activism that began in the 1870s, and in the "municipal housekeeping" movement at the turn of the century, for example.

But just as path-breaking is the editorial stance. Bloomer addresses Arthur, using her status as letter writer, magazine editor, and woman reader simultaneously. She construes herself alternately as a single self, a formal entity, and a collective speaker: her "our" means both herself formally and her readers collectively; her "we" conflates the editorial "we," in widespread use at the time, and the collective "we" increasingly used by feminist women writers. Throughout the sequence, Bloomer's position within the dynamic letter form helps her claim the authority to volley between "I" and "we," individual and collective, woman reader and professional editor, personal and political. These multiple and overlapping self-representations create an authorial position that is at once oppositional and collaborative, formal and personal, professional and independent. They construct a feminist editorial voice.

Numerous *Lily* contributors apparently followed Bloomer's lead. Increasingly through the 1850s, writers move between the hard-won "I" and the gathering, collective "we," speaking politically for themselves but also carrying forward the increasing awareness of their voices as part of a feminist community.

Other contributors apparently took away different messages from the Bloomer-Arthur confrontation. Bloomer's decoding and recoding seem to have informed subsequent reading and writing practices. The anonymous author of a March 1855 contribution, "The Printer Girls," for example, has reread, so can rewrite the sentimental-domestic plot suggestively. Janet Malcolm, desolate after the (formulaic) death of her mother, makes her way to "the city." There, rather than being deceived and deflowered, she is befriended by a dark-haired, dark-eyed young woman, the double and complement of Janet's blond and blue-eyed beauty. Together the two open a print shop and, presumably, live fulfilling, successful lives of their own thereafter.[44]

A more sophisticated story also seems indebted to Bloomer's influence. "What Can Woman Do—Or the Influence of an Example" is a September 1850 contribution to the *Lily* by Alice B. Haven Neal, a novelist and yet another woman's-rights woman who frequently found a place to speak in the popular women's magazines of her day, including the market-leading *Godey's*.[45] "What Can Woman Do" is a temperance tale told by a feminist. In a double-narrative, half political parable and half sentimental-domestic story, Neal uses the juxtaposition of competing discourses to push through a transition to new ideas of women's identities and lives. The engine of this progress is its heroine, Isabel Gray, who shades between the domestic ideal of effective virtue and the feminist ideal of action on chosen principles.

Offered a glass of wine to toast her hostess, Isabel responds "in a quick, earnest voice, which drew the attention of all" that "I will drink to Lucy with all my heart, but in water if you please."[46] Although "courtesy subdued the astonishment and remonstrance of the host and his fashionable friends," still Isabel's action "formed the topic of conversation after the ladies withdrew." Even "as they re-entered the drawing room," "the ladies" still cannot read her confusing behavior. Isabel doesn't fully belong in this story. "Why, act in such a strange way?" they ask.

Isabel's reply to these queries is cagey but clear: "How very terrible!" she exclaims, then continues: "Is it such a mighty offense?" Isabel stands firm on her temperance principles, learned from experience, as she explains: "I have seen too much of [liquor's] ill effects to agree. . . . My heart has long condemned the practice of convivial drinking, and I cannot countenance it even by *seeming* to join."

Acknowledging her visibility as both an oddity and an example, Isabel asserts that "we none of us know the influence we exert." And this night she "had a definite object in [her] pointed refusal": "young Lewis has recently made a resolution to avoid everything that can lead him to his one fault. . . . It is but very lately that he has seen what a moral and mental ruin threatened him, and has resolved to gain mastery over the temptation."

Evoking the sentimental structure, she continues: "To-night was his first trial." "I saw the struggle between custom, pride and good resolutions . . . I have spared him one stroke—he will be stronger the next time to refuse for himself," she asserts.

The women are rapt by this woman's rendering of the reformation of a male inebriate at the unspoken urging and example of a woman. They are so moved, in fact, that one guest comments to Isabel, "you should have been a novelist." Although Isabel isn't, Neal is. The author uses Isabel's story to image an involved audience that, following on a familiar formula, begins to broach the new. She uses Isabel to move beyond her.

Lewis, too, is moved by the heroine. He comments meaningfully on her positive power over him: "God bless you, Miss Gray," he murmurs. "'I confess I wavered—you made me ashamed of my weakness; I will not mind their taunting now,' was all the grateful, warm-hearted man could say." Marked by the warm sentiment and the "friendly clasp of [Isabel's] hand," Lewis and Isabel seem destined for domestic bliss.

But Neal interrupts the apparent romance plot, pursuing instead a feminist fable. To make the turn, she employs the structural device of the authorial addendum, but in a new place. Instead of positioning her political paragraph at the end of the narrative, she interjects it in the middle, signaling further development in the remainder of the story. "Ah, my sisters," she proclaims, "if you could but realize that all the beauty and grace are but talents entrusted to your keeping, and that the happiness of many may rest upon the most trivial act, you would not use that loveliness for an ignoble triumph, or so thoughtlessly tread the path of life!"

Such structured sentiments have appeared before in feminist as well as earlier women's reform magazines. But here, they are employed not as a strategic conclusion to a sentimental tale of womanly weal or woe, but as a transition within a story that wants to go further ideologically. By using a conclusory device as a transitional one, the author, Neal, pushes beyond the sentimental-domestic tradition on which she depends, just as her heroine does. And the function of the addendum is to bring her audience along with her.

As the narrative reconvenes, Isabel is centered, and is portrayed with a new authority. "Oh, Isabel," Lucy Rushton entreats, "pray advise me." Should she trust her niece's betrothal to Lewis, who claims to be reformed? Lucy asks. Should young Emily run the risk of his recidivism?

"Yes, if she chooses it," Isabel tellingly replies. "Emily is a thoughtful and sensible girl. She does not act without judgment," she has observed. "She is just the woman to be the wife of an impulsive, generous man like Lewis," Isabel asserts. "Sufficient time has elapsed to try his principles, and her companionship will strengthen them."

"And so it proved," Neal writes, abruptly shifting from the genre of the short story to that of a political parable. "It," readers must infer, is the immense "influence" of a principled woman's "example." "There are now few happier homes than the cheerful, hospitable household over which Emily Lewis presides," she writes. Merging the happy ending of this domestic plot with the unconventional conclusion of a feminist fable, Neal continues, "Isabel Gray is always a favorite guest" in this harmonious home.

As to Isabel's story, "Robert predicts she will never marry." That may also "prove so," Neal writes, "for she is not of those who would sacrifice herself for fortune, or give her hand to any man she did not thoroughly respect and sympathize with, to escape that really very tolerable fate— becoming an old maid." Apparently, Isabel has been designed for a wider, public "influence." Hers is a different destiny.

Both Emily and Isabel provide viable (if sudden) conclusions to women's stories. Each is a heroine whose goals are achieved by her inner strength and "good judgment." Isabel's powerful example—here is "influence" activated—enables both the domestic harmony of the Lewis household and the feminist independence of Isabel's own story.

In its dual conclusions, Neal's contribution promotes the positive power of female "influence" so long as women themselves claim the right to choose where and why to apply it. The story is reaching from representation to self-representation, from "female influence" to feminist empowerment. But it isn't there yet. For Isabel's uncommon agency remains curtailed in the story. It may be more instrumental than passive "influence," yet it still emanates only from her choice of what *not* to do. Moreover, although Isabel represents choice, she also remains above communal choices herself. As the parable closes, she remains solitary, and lives under the burden as much as the benefit of exemplary status.

Despite a still-curtailed concept of woman's agency, a story such as Neal's uses a popular "feminine" formula to push through a vital transition, one that promotes the evolution of new notions of women's power and place in the world. Moreover, the moral of the story has personal, political, and also social-movement implications. It accepts differences in women's goals and choices, thus creating solidarity among them, despite divergent points of view. The formulaic doubling of the two heroines, each a role model, juxtaposes gender possibilities, allowing new conceptions to cooperate with the old. Not only can new visions emerge from established constructions (as Isabel's does), but also they can coexist with these antecedents without discrediting them. Like the early American women's magazine tradition itself, it paves pathways from "femininity" toward feminism, from Sarah Hale to Amelia Bloomer, all the while affirming a historical and cultural tradition of sisterhood so crucial to its practical success.

In an authorial addendum annexed to her final letter to T.S. Arthur, Amelia Bloomer rallies her reading sisters around her as she anticipates the future trajectory of feminist-informed media activism in America:

We care not what the name, or how popular the writer, who holds up the weakness of woman to public view, so long as we have a pen to write, or a voice to speak, we shall defend our sex from such libelous imputations. Woman has too long been kept in awe, and her powers of mind and body cramped and fettered by the false ideas in regard to her sphere, and her duty which man has heretofore so successfully impressed upon the public mind. It is time she, herself, arouse, and teach him another lesson.

There is always, of course, another lesson to teach. Bloomer speaks to Arthur, but focuses outward, beyond him, to readers everywhere—and even perhaps to history itself. She declares that women will use their increasing powers in the press to write and revise gendered language and media images, thus remaking woman in the public eye and the public mind. Claiming credibility and collectivity, asserting visibility and critical voice, she is prescient in her call to reject representation by men and in favor of self-representation by pen and voice, a shift that has become a dominant strategy of feminists in American media production and politics since the rise of the Second Wave.

NOTES

1. *Lily*, December 1, 1856, p. 150.

2. Frances B. Cogan finds another model of femininity available at this time, but there is considerable scholarly agreement that the dominant gender discourse of the day remained domesticity, which had infiltrated and now pervaded popular culture, where it remained installed and widely endorsed up to the Civil War era. See Cogan, *All-American Girl: The Ideal of Real Womanhood in Mid-Nineteenth-Century America* (Athens: University of Georgia Press, 1989).

3. Marion Marzolf, *Up from the Footnote: A History of Women Journalists* (New York: Hastings House, 1977), p. 220–1.

4. Little mention of the *Mayflower* is made by scholars of the feminist press. In their anthology *The Radical Women's Press of the 1850s* (New York: Routledge, 1991), editors Ann Russo and Cheris Kramarae only briefly describe that it was "a semi-monthly devoted to the interests of women." In "Nineteenth-Century Suffrage Periodicals," an article in William Solomon and Robert Chesney, eds., *Ruthless Criticism: New Perspectives in U.S. Communication History* (Minneapolis: University of Minnesota Press, 1993), Linda Steiner notes merely that it was more congenial to "true women" of the time since it emphasized "chaste literature, happy homes, and purity." Steiner spends more time on the *Mayflower* in her unpublished dissertation, "The Woman's Suffrage Press, 1850–1900: A Cultural Analysis" (University of Illinois at Urbana-Champaign, 1979), pp. 130–1.

5. See Marzolf, *Up from the Footnote*, p. 221.

6. Ibid., p. 222–3. See also Russo and Kramarae, eds., *The Radical Women's Press of the 1850s*, p. 11–2.

7. Russo and Cheris Kramarae, eds., *The Radical Women's Press of the 1850s*, p. 2. See, for example, Martha Solomon, ed., *A Voice of Their Own: The Woman Suffrage Press, 1840–1910* (Tuscaloosa: University of Alabama Press, 1991) and Maurine H. Beasley and Sheila J. Gibbons, *Taking Their Place: A Documentary History of Women and Journalism* (Washington, DC: The American University Press, 1993).

8. The circulations of these popular women's magazines continued to rise after the Civil War. *Godey's* proclaimed circulation in 1860 was 150,000; by 1869, the magazine claimed 500,000 readers. *Peterson's* circulation came closest to *Godey's* in the 1850s, and probably exceeded it by the Civil War. Patricia Okker provides these figures in *Our Sister Editors: Sarah J. Hale and the Tradition of Nineteenth-Century American Women Editors* (Athens: University of Georgia Press,

1995), pp. 56–7. The immense (even if exaggerated) circulations were helped by improving print technologies, and were aided by the Post Office Act of 1852, which reduced postage rates dramatically and allowed postage payment at offices of mailing.

9. Patricia Okker has identified more than 600 nineteenth-century American women periodical editors at work in the nineteenth century, many of whom began their careers in the 1840s and '50s. See *Our Sister Editors*. Okker perhaps overstates the case somewhat, as she includes in her accounting women who were involved, but who did not clearly have masthead and/or management roles. She also includes women who edited highly specialized publications and the organs of local organizations. The inclusion of these women is appropriate to her project of outlining the extent of women's editorial activity in the nineteenth century, but it exaggerates to some degree the explosive power of the somewhat fewer women who edited influential and/or national publications.

10. The women's magazine circulation figures are given by Frank Luther Mott, *A History of American Magazines, Vol. 2: 1825–1850* (New York: D. Appleton and Co., 1932), p. 41. Okker provides the national average in *Our Sister Editors*, p. 56.

11. Although some major magazines of the 1850s, notably *Harper's*, eschewed advertising (save for notices of its own books), low rates (on average, $20 per octavo page; $.15 per line) did gradually encourage advertisers to consider buying magazine space. *Godey's* and *Peterson's* ran between five and ten pages of advertising per issue at this time; the *Lily* and its contemporaries generally ran few if any advertisements, and Aldrich's *Genius of Liberty*, as noted, accepted none.

12. Barbara Welter, "The Cult of True Womanhood, 1820–1860," *American Quarterly*, vol. 18, no. 2 (summer 1966), pp. 151–74.

13. See Pauline Wright Davis, "Not a Ladies' Magazine," *Una*, February 1, 1853, p. 4. See also Mary Warrington, "Two Political Parties: 'Ladies' and 'Women,'" *Lily*, August 1, 1856, p. 110.

14. See, for example, "The Dying Mother," *Lily*, June 1849, p. 48; "The Mother," *Lily*, June 1854, p. 57. The "fascination with death and mourning" is seen as definitive by Ann Douglas in *The Feminization of American Culture* (New York: Doubleday, 1988), pp. 200–7.

15. Although biographical information about Vaughan is surprisingly scarce, it is known that Vaughan's opposition to Elizabeth Cady Stanton and Susan B. Anthony at the first Woman's New York State Temperance Society convention caused the two to withdraw from both the society and the temperance movement overall after 1853. In addition, Vaughan is known to have coedited, with Linus Brockett, *Women's Work in the Civil War: A Record of Heroism, Patriotism and Patience* (Philadelphia: Zeigler, McCurdy, 1867). A short story, "Fruits of Sorrow, or an Old Maid's Story," is in Sandra Koppelman, *Old Maids: Short Stories by Nineteenth Century U.S. Women Writers* (London: Pandora Press, 1984).

16. See Lori Ginzberg, *Women and the Work of Benevolence: Morality, Politics and Class in the Nineteenth-Century United States* (New Haven: Yale University Press, 1990), p. 114–5.

17. Mary C. Vaughan, "Maternal Influence," *Lily*, February 1851, p. 11.

18. This structure was also used by conservative writers, seeking to move women back to conventional understandings of gender and their place in the home. An 1854 *Una* contributor submitted for the purposes of rebuttal an article by the sentimental-domestic author Mrs. Sigourney that had used this strategic structure. Sigourney asserted that "true nobility of woman is to keep her own sphere and to adorn it; not like the comet, daunting and perplexing other systems, but as the pure star, which is the first to light the day, and last to leave it." Her authorial addendum turns to readers, calling out, "Mothers! Are not our rights sufficiently extensive—the sanctuary of love, the throne of the heart, the moulding of the whole mass of mind... have we not power enough in all realms of sorrow and suffering—over all forms of ignorance and want—amid all ministrations of love, from the cradle dream to the sepulcher." See Mary F. Love, "Mrs. Sigourney on Women's Rights," *Una*, June 1854, p. 282.

19. See Mary Ryan, *The Empire of the Mother: American Writing About Domesticity 1830–1860* (New York: Harrington Park Press, 1985), p. 77. See also Lori Ginzberg, *Women and the Work of Benevolence*, pp. 113–5.

20. The *Advocate* at this time was under the editorship of Sarah Towne Smith Martyn (dates not available), a temperance and moral reform activist and editor. Martyn later edited the *Olive Plant and Ladies' Temperance Advocate* (1841–42) as well as the *True Advocate* and the *White Banner* during the 1840s. She retired from moral reform work to edit her own women's magazine, the *Ladies Wreath* (1846–55), a $1/year, thirty-six-page New York monthly that claimed a circulation of 25,000 at the height of its popularity in 1853. The *Wreath* was later edited by Helen Irving, wife of the nephew and biographer of Washington Irving, between 1856 and 1862.

21. Cited by Mary Ryan in *The Empire of the Mother: American Writing about Domesticity 1830–1860* (New York: Harrington Park Press, 1985), p. 77.

22. Several early feminists active in the *Lily* and other women's magazines, such Frances Dana Barker Gage (1808–84), published temperance tales in conjunction with their reform activities. Gage published *Elsie Magoon*, a temperance novel, in 1867, the same year that she published a collection of sentimental verse, *Poems*. The mother of eight children, Gage was also a frequent contributor to the *Ladies Repository* (1841–76) of Cincinnati, Ohio.

23. Mary Ryan, *The Cult of the Mother: American Writing About Domesticity 1830–1860* (New York: Harrington Park Press, 1985).

24. The contribution, including the references to these sources, is available in Russo and Kramarae, eds., *The Radical Women's Press of the 1850s*, pp. 155–6.

25. Oakes Smith (1806–93) wrote poems, sketches, and short pieces for a host of women's magazines, including *Godey's* and *Lady's Companion* (1834–44), and

for literary magazines, including *Graham's* (1826–58), and the *Southern Literary Messenger* (1835–59). She also published a series of women's rights articles in Greeley's *New York Tribune*, later collected as *Woman and Her Needs* (1851). Her *Hints on Dress and Beauty* (1852) was shortly followed by an odd, feminist-leaning novel, *Bertha and Lily* (1854), which tells the tale of a woman of apparently superior character who, after being seduced, bears a child out of wedlock, only to lose the baby during a period of "madness." She later coedited a short-lived literary magazine, *Great Republican Monthly* (1859).

26. Some subsequent contributions also display this pattern. "Woman's Sphere," an April 1855 contribution by "Marita," works in a strictly secular argument, and even interpolates a courtroom format to press part of her case, before she concludes, "But hearken, a voice is sounding through the land, 'woman fulfill thy destiny'. . . . Put forth the full powers of thy being and reap the fruit. Study thine own capacities, and for whatsoever thou findest thyself capacitated to do, let it be done, for all may be encompassed by woman which is by man encompassed. For her there is no circumscribed sphere. Let each and every woman seek out the work designed for her accomplishment, and when it shall be done, then will woman have fulfilled her mission." See the *Lily*, April 1855, pp. 71–2.

27. See Stephen Botein, "'Meer Mechanics' and an Open Press: The Business and Political Strategies of Colonial American Printers," *Perspectives in American History*, vol. 9 (1975), pp. 126–225. See also Lawrence Leder, "The Role of Newspapers in Early America 'In Defense of Their Own Liberty,'" *Huntington Library Quarterly*, vol. 30, no. 1 (November 1966), pp. 1–16.

28. Arthur M. Schlesinger, *Prelude to Independence: The Newspaper War in Britain, 1746–1776* (New York: Alfred A. Knopf, 1958). See also Michael Lund, *America's Continuing Story: An Introduction to Serial Fiction, 1850–1900* (Detroit: Wayne State University Press, 1993), p. 16.

29. Okker, *Our Sister Editors*, p. 31.

30. See Linda Steiner, "Finding Community in Nineteenth-Century Suffrage Periodicals." *American Journalism*, vol. 1, no. 1 (summer 1983), pp. 1–15. See also Linda Steiner, "Nineteenth-Century Suffrage Periodicals: Conceptions of Womanhood and the Press," in William Solomon and Robert W. Chesney, eds., *Ruthless Criticism: New Perspectives in U.S. Communication History* (Minneapolis: University of Minnesota Press, 1993).

31. Okker explains that the sense of sisterly connections drew strength from popular gender ideas about woman's instincts for nurture and group support, one reason this notion thrived, structuring popular women's magazines throughout the nineteenth century. See *Our Sister Editors*, p. 22.

32. Swisshelm insisted on Dr. Johnson's spelling.

33. Frances Dana Barker Gage (1808–84) had a limited education and eight children to raise, so she wrote letters to newspapers and articles for magazines, often about the links between temperance, abolition, and women's rights. With

her husband in failing health, a move to Columbus, Ohio, resulted in her taking an associate editor position with the *Ohio Cultivator* (1845–66), a farm and family magazine, and later with *Field Notes* (1861–62), an agricultural paper.

34. Okker makes this argument in *Our Sister Editors*.

35. Belle Ville, "Woman's Sphere," *Lily*, September 15, 1854, pp. 135–6.

36. See Nancy Cott, *The Grounding of Modern Feminism* (New Haven: Yale University Press, 1987). See also Janet Zollinger Giele, *Two Paths to Women's Equality: Temperance, Suffrage, and the Origins of Modern Feminism* (New York: Twayne Publishers, 1995).

37. Belle Ville, "Woman's Sphere," *Lily*, November 15, 1854, p. 168.

38. Ibid., January 15, 1855, p. 28.

39. See Nina Baym's overview in the chapter "Classes of Novels," in *Novels, Readers, and Reviewers: Responses to Fiction in Antebellum America* (Ithaca: Cornell University Press, 1984), pp. 202–7.

40. Amelia Bloomer (1818–94) helped organize the Ladies Temperance Society in Seneca Falls that launched the *Lily*. After 1852, when Bloomer alone edited and published the magazine, it became an influential journal advocating a range of women's rights reforms and its offices a central meeting place for women in the area. Bloomer's 1851 editorial in the *Lily* advocating the wearing of the Turkish-style pants outfit that would soon, in ridicule, bear her name, brought notoriety to the costume and a surge in subscriptions to the magazine. After moving to Ohio with her husband, and giving over the *Lily* to Mary B. Birdsall, former women's department editor of the *Indiana Farmer* (1851–61), Bloomer and her husband owned and edited the *Western Home Visitor* (1853–55).

41. [Amelia Bloomer], "Ruling a Wife," *Lily*, November 1850, pp. 86–7.

42. Letter writing continues to be an important subject in women's magazines through the nineteenth century, appearing as the topic of articles in such best-sellers as the *Ladies' Home Journal*, *Demorest's Monthly*, and the *Delineator*. Harvey Green discusses the continuing importance of letter writing in a middle-class lady's life in the nineteenth century in *The Light of the Home: An Intimate View of the Lives of Women in Victorian America* (New York: Pantheon Books, 1983).

43. Karen Halttunen discusses this popular trope, and argues that it reflects a crisis of social identity between women and men in a culture destabilized by enormous social, geographic, and economic shifts. See Karen Halttunen, *Confidence Men and Painted Women: A Study of Middle-Class Culture in America 1830–1870* (New Haven: Yale University Press, 1982).

44. "The Printer Girls," *Lily*, March 1855, p. 38. This scenario is evocative of the configurations of the same-sex friendships between woman-identified women that Carol Smith-Rosenberg has described in her germinal article "The Female World of Love and Ritual: Relations Between Women in Nineteenth Century America." The piece first appeared in the premiere issue of *Signs*, vol. 1, no. 1 (1975). It was later reprinted in her *Disorderly Conduct: Visions of Gender in Victorian America* (New York: Alfred A. Knopf, 1985).

45. "Cousin Alice" (1827–63), as she was pseudonymously known, met her husband through her frequent publication of stories in his magazine, *Neal's Saturday Gazette and Lady's Literary Museum* (1836–53). Her novels include *Helen Morton's Trial* (1849); *The Gossips of Rivertown* (1850), a biting commentary she famously regretted having published; *No Such Word as Fail* (1852); and *Patient Waiting No Loss* (1853). Her last novel, *The Good Report,* was published posthumously in 1867.

46. Alice B. Neal, "What Can Woman Do—or, the Influence of an Example," *Lily,* September 1850, pp. 65–7.

EPILOGUE

Where Are They Now? Women's Voices and the Mass Market Magazine

The first feminist magazines realized the political promises of the American magazine perhaps more fully than had any women's publications before. And few would ever again. Mainstream, mass-market women's magazines did spearhead numerous political crusades in the decades to come—leading charges for pure food and drug laws, child welfare legislation, and false advertising protections, for example[1]—but not until the magazines of the Second Wave were the capabilities of the American magazine again plied in specific pursuit of women's rights.

And getting there was an uphill battle. After the Civil War, almost everything changed in the world of magazines. The literary marketplace grew more developed and sophisticated beginning in the 1870s, and women's magazines especially both reflected and advanced the emerging American mass market. Magazines (and newspapers) run by individual printers, lone "literary ladies," or small communities of social activists largely vanished. Instead, periodical publication became the province of technologically developing, profit-seeking companies with increasingly professional editorial staffs, defined occupational structures, and regularized features and departments.

As conventional wisdom would have it, such regulated production closed out the opportunities for resistance and response so vital to the early magazines' politics and influence. The standard story holds that the emerging mass-market women's magazine virtually blanketed the woman reader's world with tailored, homogenized messages created with somebody else's interests at heart. The newfangled magazines supposedly sold-out their readers, using a century of trust and participation as a means of marshalling millions of women and delivering them to aggressive national advertisers like so many sheep to the wolves.

Yet that is not exactly what happened.

MASS-MARKET MIND-SET: THE MODERN AMERICAN WOMEN'S MAGAZINE

Spurred by an economic boom, American publishing became a national industry in the decades after the Civil War. The localism, regionalism, and sectionalism that had characterized the antebellum economy began to give way under the nationalizing forces of industrialization, improving transportation, increasing population, and rising real per capita income.[2] At the same time, cultural changes critical to the industry, including rising literacy rates, faster and lower-cost printing technologies, reduced paper prices, and favorable postage rates, made possible the first truly national magazines and newspapers America had ever seen.[3]

The mass-market magazines in general, and women's magazines in particular, were less literary and less elite than were their antebellum predecessors. Handy, practical, cheap, and easy to read, the newfangled magazines spoke to a wider range of women and about more concrete and consumerist issues. Whatever their intellectual and literary shortcomings, the mass-market women's magazines quickly surpassed their suddenly high-brow-looking predecessors in popularity.[4] And they have never looked back.

The new mass-market magazines were addressed to growing urban middle-class audiences who, according to one scholar, had been "untouched by, untroubled by, and uninterested in the literary monthlies."[5] Mass-market magazines pursued these untapped readers with unprecedented focus and intention. They instituted new levels of editorial control in a drive to target specific needs and issues and to manage the heterogeneity of reader response. They began to routinize distinctions between readers and writers, segregating reader comments into "correspondence" sections. The age of the amateur contributor was passing; soon readers were invited to write articles, stories, or poetry for magazines mainly as part of special contests—and many of these were sponsored by advertisers, not editors.[6] The new magazines slowly began to increase the proportion of nonfiction fare, favoring the editorial control and topical targeting this mode offered over and against the more polysemic possibilities of fiction. Although stories and serials remained a notable element of the mix in women's magazines particularly, they were increasingly obtained by contract with book publishers. This arrangement promoted an emerging "star system," with its tendencies toward favoritism for market-friendly expressions. Overall, magazine producers wanted very much to move away from amateur writers, active readers, contradictions and debate, pushing instead toward professionally authored articles quoting experts (most of them men) to create a smoother, safer, more circumscribed environment amenable to advertisers.[7]

Such efforts to manage the democratic dynamics of the magazine to suit the rationalizing, nationalizing marketplace have generally been seen as almost perfectly successful in the case of women's magazines. The "masculine" interests, patriarchal control and marketplace profit, are imagined to have operated in perfect sync, hand in glove. Richard Ohmann's essay "Where Did Mass Culture Come From? The Case of Magazines," the basis for his *Selling Culture: Magazines, Markets and Class at the Turn of the Century* (1996), argues that mass-market women's magazines effectively performed a gatekeeping function, overseeing the passage of women readers into the new world of consumer capitalism.[8] The magazines "contributed to ideological domination," suggests another scholar, by setting and enforcing hegemonic limits on people's social identities and leisure choices.[9] The mass-market women's magazines created status insecurity and dependence on mostly male professional advice, Christopher Wilson concludes, circumstances that served the twin interests of patriarchy and profit-making.[10]

These analyses have in common the conception of the mass-market magazine as little more than the mouthpiece of male interests, and its female readership as passive dupes of these designs. Still, some of them have reminded us that despite anticipatory production and targeted hegemonic limits, the inherent multiplicity of the American magazine form still left "ample room for diversity."[11] And certainly mass-market magazines could not have so perfectly entrapped women in consumerist dependency so quickly, since the advertising industry was not fully organized until after 1917, when the American Association of Advertising Agencies was founded.[12] Nevertheless, the consensus remains that mass-market women's magazines into the present day have betrayed and co-opted unsuspecting readers, and have done so with near-perfect efficiency—expertly, single-mindedly and without the slightest conflict, undertow, or fear of failure.

COMPETING CAVEATS: GENDER, COMMERCE, AND THE RISE OF THE MASS-MARKET WOMEN'S MAGAZINE

As the mass-market women's magazines began to achieve success at the turn of the twentieth century, setting many formal standards for both the rhetorical and presentation strategies that still prevail in the field, competing voices remained the order of the day. Although women's magazine publishers were leaders in the emerging field of market research,[13] editors, then and now, were given considerable latitude about content. They were hired for their editorial instincts, and were generally asked to trust them. That is, with one caveat: "so long as circulations were increasing."[14]

Yet an editor's instincts and the goal of circulation increases could all too easily be at odds, especially where mass-market women's magazines were concerned. For the better part of the past 100 years, the top sellers—including *Ladies' Home Journal* (begun 1883), *Delineator* (1873–1937), *Woman's Home Companion* (1874–1957), and *Good Housekeeping* (begun 1885)—were edited by men. In fact, this male dominance provoked the storied 1970 sit-in at the offices of John Mack Carter, then the *Ladies' Home Journal*'s editor in chief. A cadre of feminists occupied the offices, demanding greater opportunity and upward mobility for women staffers. Nevertheless, it wasn't until the 1980s that most leading women's magazines had a woman at the helm.

As we have seen, men have edited and published women's magazines from the beginning, yet that doesn't mean they have always had clear-cut control. In fact, from the start male editors were both the masters and the servants of their female audiences. And this already complicated relationship grew more vexed with the rise of the mass market.

As editors, these men negotiated a widely shifting set of gendered pressures at the turn of the century. To keep circulation increasing, male editors were pressed to continually expand their address to women and to widen the range of ideas and interests the magazines entertained. At the same time, male editors also saw it in their interest to limit language and coverage, emphasizing certain ideas and options. A focus on women's interests as housewives, mothers and consumers bolstered advertising potential and perhaps their own sense of themselves as professionals, as bosses—and indeed as men.

The rapid change and high stakes that characterized the postwar expansion to national markets made such collisions even more problematic. Commercial expansion in the magazine industry created intense competition among increasing numbers of sophisticated and potentially profitable players.[15] Where there is industry change and marketplace competition, not to mention shifts in women's status, "masculinity" is under even more pressure to prove itself.[16] Such forces fomented internal complication in mass-market women's magazines—complications that, in a vicious cycle, intensified the very pressures from which they sprang.

The "masculine" expertise defined and demanded by the new mass marketplace disdained male uncertainty as both unmanly and unprofessional.[17]

Within this gender-sensitive frame, the masculine interests of patriarchy and profits often went in different directions, at times leaving male editors at odds with their audiences, their advertisers, and themselves.

Some effects of these conflicts can be read in magazine content. Take the *Ladies' Home Journal*, the standard-bearer of the era. Launched in 1883 by the publisher Cyrus Curtis and edited to early success by his wife, Louisa Knapp Curtis, the *Journal* was a prototype of the American mass-market magazine generally, and the mass-market women's magazine specifically. What Sarah Hale's magazines were to the nineteenth-century magazine,[18] the *Journal* was to the twentieth. The *Journal* was the first American magazine to circulate widely and cheaply by dint of a significant revenue stream from advertising, the first magazine to surpass one million in paid circulation (in 1903).[19] It was also the first to attempt to turn the intimacy, trust, and collective participation by which the women's magazine tradition had been built to the pursuit of profits. Curtis sensed early on that these qualities could be valuable in contextualizing advertising and in pitching products to women readers.

Although it was Knapp who put the *Journal* on the map, it was former adman Edward Bok who was given the helm as the magazine headed for the mass-market super-stardom after 1889.[20] Unlike Knapp, Bok was a staunch conservative on gender issues; his editorials were filled with his reverence for domesticity and his disdain for new opportunities and freedoms in middle-class women's lives.[21] As Helen Damon-Moore explains, Bok "marshalled religious forces in his magazine, calling on ministers to assert the God-ordained basis of traditional gender roles, and to chastise women who dared challenge God's plan."[22]

But Bok's outspoken efforts to roll back women's gains, and his rallying of time-tested authorities to pronounce delimiting prescriptions about women's roles, were repeatedly challenged by the new commercial imperative to augment audiences—an achievement that, in turn, would promote his "masculine" status as it boosted his profits and professional success. The editor's patriarchal desires, that is to say, were often countermanded by his "masculine" professional ambitions. As a result, Bok was pushed to succumb to the counterclaims of the market, to swallow his patriarchal preferences in the face of women readers' demands. He frequently incorporated new departments and columns in the *Journal* because that's what it took to bring women readers in and to keep them coming back for more.

Bok carried columns about women's work outside the home throughout the 1880s, for example. This was a necessary compromise with reader interests and related marketplace demands. As Alice Kessler-Harris has written, middle-class married women—his readership—was the fastest-growing group of workers in America after 1880.[23] Although, as Damon-Moore explains, "Bok and his writers joined . . . other periodicals in their anxiety about such developments,"[24] the editor in chief was not in a position to hold out against the burgeoning interests of his audience. Bok admitted "that his 'breadwinner' and 'dressing for business' columns, among others, had been created in direct response" to reader demand.[25] Later, he again bowed to reader pressure on women's suffrage, which he agreed to explore in a regular column on the workings of government.[26]

The tension between Bok's personal proclivity to contract and the commercial necessity to expand ideas about women's roles can be seen within individual columns as well. Very often, the periodical pressures that had helped previous magazine editors and readers move into new realms also pushed Bok to open his pages to new possibilities for women. The early column on women's work remains a strong illustration. At first, the column presented fantasy businesses with little realistic potential to produce a serious income. The premiere topic? "Caring for Poultry." Subsequent columns proposed such unlikely means of earning a living as "Bee Keeping" and the "Raising of Silkworms." These topics may have reflected the *Journal*'s audience base in the Midwest, with its agricultural mind-set. Still, the likelihood that such pursuits would result in reliable moneymaking anywhere in the country seems small. However, as months went by, the column began to address more plausible business ventures, and ones that might well be pursued by readers across the country. Over time, columns on catering, organized child care, floral design, retailing, and the restaurant business appeared.

These fields remain gendered to be sure—hegemonic limits were hardly exploded as a result of these pressures. Yet boundaries did move in gender-transgressive directions insofar as these columns helped make women's financial independence both possible and permissible. And the mass-market mind-set may again be seen as a prime mover. To get and keep the readers advertisers wanted, *Journal* editors were pushed to explore new angles, new ideas, issue after issue, month after month. This need for the new in what was a maturing market for popular women's magazines effectively pushed the *Journal* to acknowledge, address, and authorize new roles and realms for women.

From there, broader marketplace conditions further promoted widening horizons. The *Journal* was the leader in the field as the mass-market women's magazine took shape, so, not surprisingly, competitors frequently imitated it. The *Woman's Home Companion* followed the *Journal's* lead, for example, soon launching a regular "Careers" column, which ran until the magazine's demise in 1957. The *Delineator*, another rival, later launched a work column of its own. Even *Good Housekeeping*, the quintessential homemaker's magazine, started a "Woman's Work and Wages" column after 1890. And thereafter, *Good Housekeeping* integrated women's work into its total editorial vision. The magazine ran such columns as "The Working Woman's Home" and "Fashions for Work" in subsequent years.[27]

ADVERTISING: AN UNSTABLE ALLY

And when it came to advertising content, collisions also occurred. A fair amount of mass-market women's magazine advertising actually argued against patriarchy, against containment or control of women readers' lives, because that was the way to sales.

After all, not all consumer products are meant to be used by middle-class women in the home. For example, as Ellen Garvey has revealed, among the products that were advertised most heavily in turn-of-the-century women's magazines was the bicycle.[28] By necessity, to generate sales of this product, bicycle ads promoted women's autonomy and independence. Although patriarchal powers heavily inveighed against these aspects of bicycle riding, advertisers made only modest concessions to them (in reshaping seats, for example). And they kept on pushing their products to women, rarely refraining from visual or rhetorical emphasis on freedom, fashionable fun, and independence—because that's what they thought would work. (And they were right.)

But even advertising for household appliances often looked well beyond the white picket fence. Many ads bespoke women's desire for liberty—or at least nodded to this hope—by emphasizing freedom from housework. An 1896 ad in the *Ladies' Home Journal*, for instance, proclaimed, "Don't Sweep the Old Way! The New Woman sweeps hard and soft carpets, bare floors, with a Sweeperette." Whatever "ironies" the supposedly labor-saving devices may have introduced into women's domestic lives,[29] their advertising subtly courted women's identification with movements for independence, and played on their presumed desires for a freer relationship with the home.

Such political rhetoric grew more pronounced over time. A 1910 ad in the *Ladies' Home Journal* for Old Dutch Cleanser claimed to be a "champion of women's rights," including the right to "freedom from household drudgery" and "the right to spotless floors . . . without the penalty of an aching back." A 1914 ad in the *Journal* promised to "revolutionize" women's life and work, announcing that the Sturlevant vacuum cleaner was a prime mover in the creation of "Woman in Her Newer Sphere." Although Bonnie Fox has argued that the "radical appeal of liberation from domestic labor was evident only in the early part of the [twentieth] century" because it raised "the possibility that women's interests might lie outside the confines of domesticity,"[30] this language appeared earlier and stayed in force longer than she allows. Women's magazine advertising used "new woman" imagery and a rhetoric of individuality and independence at least into the 1930s.

And it reappeared not long after that. Advertiser deployments of such political rhetoric cropped up occasionally during the war years and into the 1940s, and it re-emerged beginning in the 1960s. The well-known "You've Come a Long Way, Baby" slogan for Virginia Slims cigarettes in the 1970s is the modern poster-child for the long history of political language in product advertising for women. On the one hand, such pitches, like their ancestors at the turn of the century, appropriated political rhetoric for commercial gain. Such rhetorical mergers seem to suggest that a woman's power in public amounts to little more than her consumerist choices in the marketplace—what might be called "commodity feminism."[31] After all, before 1920, the only real "vote" a woman had was as a consumer selecting among product choices; later, her hard-won public voice was partly channeled into the marketplace, where she could "endorse" what is worthy in America by choosing to purchase it.

All this is true. But what is simultaneously true is that such advertising also brought political language home to millions of mass-market women's magazine readers through the twentieth century. Indeed, since advertising came to occupy so prominent and highlighted a place in popular women's magazines, the political gist might have appeared to be endorsed by the considerable clout the magazines had with their audiences. It all depends on readers: the mixed messages of such advertising could have undermined women's actual political interests and involvement— or worked to legitimate and encourage them.

Recall that readers encountered these ads as one voice among many in the mass-market women's magazine. As Jennifer Scanlon has brought to light, the *Ladies' Home Journal*, the trendsetter, was a "mishmash of professional advice and helpful hints from various points of view, directed at a variety of audiences."[32] When it came to women's work outside the home, for instance, the *Journal* "provided a host of arguments . . . some favored women's employment, others deplored the very notion of women leaving the household arena, and still others accepted the inevitable and suggested ways of accommodating to . . . the accompanying social changes."[33] The same was true when it came to housekeeping, dating, education, and fashion. A reader "might have been shocked into a realization of the evils of fashion while reading an article, 'The Plain Country Woman,'" Scanlon notes, "but had only to turn to the next page to be enticed in the opposite direction by an article entitled 'What I See in New York,' which outlined the latest styles."[34] Even magazine fiction, which critics from Friedan on down have castigated as foreclosing women's imaginative possibilities, "invite subversive as well as prescriptive readings," Scanlon finds.[35] In this context, the political rhetoric of advertising might be seen to have simply carried the discourse and the issues to the table, giving millions of middle-class American women readers the opportunity to take it, leave it, or run with it as they saw fit.

The mass-market women's magazine is generally seen as rather a secret agent for the masculine interests of patriarchy and profit. But a closer look suggests disruptions that have not typically been seen. Gender ideology—especially masculinity—may have played a vexing role. Patriarchy and commercialism have not always worked hand in glove. And last, but not least, the American magazine has always been a dynamic form, wherein various pressures, voices, and forces are continually at play. Multiple readings, therefore, are always available; meanings, implications and outcomes are always to some extent up for grabs. This principle remains pertinent to this day. The modern, sophisticated mass-market magazine of the twenty-first century still cannot blot out the democratic dynamics and audience agencies that have always been the soul of the women's magazine form—and succeed.

This gloss cannot begin to recover all the lost voices of the early women's magazines or to capture all the complexities of the genre in its mass-market form. Nor can it effectively suggest all that the modern women's magazine has become today. But this history of the genre as far as it goes does reveal some of the powers, projects, and politics that have been missing from view—and that could be of use.

For one thing, a less stable, less easy vision of gender order in American women's magazines must come into view. From its origins, the genre could not rest easily with patriarchal control or reader domination. Its very survival and success has depended on dialogue, on an ongoing process of contribution and response, expression, renovation, repetition and revision over time. The magazine's formal qualities, discursive practices, classic audience and public image have all supported that process from the start, so even those producers who wanted to control the conversation have often failed, at least partly, in their designs.

At the same time, a less divided vision of women's culture becomes available. That culture is still strongly segmented by race and also by social class to be sure. But white, middle-class women's communities of the Left and Right can now be seen as more intimately allied than has previously been acknowledged. The now-visible continuum between early popular women's magazines and the first feminist periodicals in America suggests that women who came from divergent political positions in fact borrowed from one another, and variously depended on one another, in the historical drive to claim visibility and voice in public. The women's magazine was a crucial site and vehicle of that cooperation, promoting the circulation of language and ideas, inviting the exchange and feedback, and advertising the process and productions of such collective work before the public eye. Thus, this first form of women's popular culture let an influential cohort of women constitute themselves as a bona fide and potentially powerful public, innovating identities, language, and stories that created new possibilities for all women's real lives in America.

To acknowledge the ways in which the early women's magazines helped women imagine and organize themselves in the pursuit of wider opportunities in the American public is not to say that magazine "democracy" can pass or should for actual political participation. As Bonnie Dow has aptly written in her study of television feminism in prime time, "images can and have contributed to the [women's rights] struggle, but they cannot substitute for it."[36] In rescuing the discursive, narrative, imaginative, and also cultural advances assisted by women's work within their miscellaneous magazines, we must guard against mistaking these accomplishments for anything more than they are.

But we must take care not to underestimate them, or the women involved, either. If this examination of the dynamics of early American women's magazines brings one women's issue forward, it is this: the vilification-victimization schema of women's magazines and media more generally has run its course. We can no longer write off women's magazines as merely a "feminine" formula—because we've seen that, over time, editors, writers, and readers have used numerous "feminine" conventions to press new claims for equal opportunity and cultural empowerment. In fact, the feminist discourse that founded the American women's movement might have been lost without them. Neither can we dismiss the genre because its many male makers may have intended to corral and co-opt women. From the start, some of these strategies simply backfired. And many others failed or fell short because women participants in magazine communities revised or resisted them, insisting—through whatever channels remained available to them—that their magazines should attempt to serve their interests and needs. Women's magazine readers, even the less-educated popular readers of old, have demonstrated time and again that women do have minds of their own.

Perhaps the still-available pleasures of personal authority and participatory agency—not to mention the just plain fun of meandering at whim through a miscellaneous text where women are the subject of every story—have helped make the women's magazine so popular for so long. Even today, women's magazines invite audiences to read episodically, personally, superficially, imaginatively, and responsively as they choose. And they still do what the first versions did: ask and allow women to create their own experiences of the text, their own master narratives every time through. Even though delimited or temporary, such agency and involvements challenge and champion women's subjectivities, collectivities, and creativity in ways that have never yet been available elsewhere.

By recognizing the collaboration past readers and writers have managed—despite the many absences, limitations and attenuations of the women's magazine space—we may even see clues to a more inclusive feminism, a more inviting American women's movement moving forward. We readers might thereby be the ones to grasp some of the original public potential of the American women's magazine, and ply it toward the inclusive progress we need in this postmodern and purportedly postfeminist age.

And if something like that happens, maybe then we can finally let go of the guilt.

NOTES

1. Kathleen L. Endres, "Muckraking: A Term Worth Redefining," *American Journalism*, vol. 14, no. 3-4 (1997), pp. 333-35.

2. The literature on industrialization and modernization is extensive. The noted elements are drawn from Alan Trachtenberg, *The Incorporation of America: Culture and Society in the Gilded Age* (New York: Hill & Wang, 1982) and Susan Strasser, *Satisfaction Guaranteed: The Making of the American Mass Marketplace* (New York: Pantheon Books, 1989).

3. The professional organizing that was occurring in the publishing industry at this time is denoted by the launch of *Publishers Weekly*, in New York, in 1872.

4. Helen Damon-Moore discusses the ascendancy of the mass-market women's magazine over its elite literary predecessors, such as *Godey's*, in *Magazines for the Millions: Gender and Commerce in the Ladies' Home Journal and the Saturday Evening Post, 1880–1910* (Albany: State University of New York Press, 1994), p. 22.

5. Samuel Playsted Wood, *The Story of Advertising* (New York: Donald Press Company, 1949), p. 202.

6. Ellen Guber Garvey discusses this use of games and contests in *The Adman in the Parlor: Magazines and the Gendering of Consumer Culture* (New York: Oxford University Press, 1996).

7. "As they moved towards preplanning, commissioning, and internal staff," Christopher Wilson explains, mass-market magazines "were becoming increasingly less the province of the nonaffiliated, voluntary contributor . . . but active agents in a managed market." Christopher Wilson, *The Labor of Words: Literary Professionalism in the Progressive Era* (Athens, GA: University of Georgia Press, 1985), p. 53.

8. See Richard Ohmann, *Selling Culture: Magazines, Markets, and Class at the Turn of the Century* (New York: Verso Books, 1996).

9. Matthew Schneirov, *The Dream of a New Social Order: Popular Magazines in America 1893–1914* (New York: Columbia University Press, 1994), p. 7.

10. Christopher P. Wilson, "The Rhetoric of Consumption: Mass-Market Magazines and the Demise of the Gentle Reader 1880–1920," in Richard Wightman Fox and T.J. Jackson Lears, eds., *The Culture of Consumption: Critical Essays in American History, 1880–1980* (New York: Pantheon Books, 1983), pp. 39–64.

11. Schneirov, *The Dream of a New Social Order*, pp. 10–1.

12. Ibid., p. 10.

13. Mary Ellen Zuckerman offers a detailed discussion of market research innovations by American women's magazine publishers in *A History of Popular Women's Magazines in the United States, 1792–1995* (Westport, CT: Greenwood Press, 1998).

14. Schneirov, *The Dream of a New Social Order*, p. 10.

15. See Zuckerman, *A History of Popular Women's Magazines in the United States 1792–1995*.

16. See Michael Kimmel, *Manhood in America* (New York: The Free Press, 1996).

17. Schneirov, *The Dream of a New Social Order*, pp. 10–1.

18. See Patricia Okker, *Our Sister Editors: Sarah J. Hale and the Tradition of Nineteenth-Century Women Editors* (Athens: University of Georgia Press, 1995).

19. Damon-Moore, *Magazines for the Millions*, p. 1.

20. Bok authored a number of books, several of which are autobiographical in character. His most renowned is *The Americanization of Edward Bok: The Autobiography of a Dutch Boy Fifty Years Later* (New York: Charles Scribner's Sons, 1923). However, two other of his books represent him as the model American

male: *Successward: A Young Man's Book for Young Men* (New York: Charles Scribner's Sons, 1896) and *Why I Believe in Poverty as the Richest Experience That Can Come to a Boy* (New York: Houghton Mifflin, 1915).

21. Bok's conservative politics with regard to women is the subject of Michael Dennis Hummel, "The Attitudes of Edward Bok and the Ladies' Home Journal Toward Women's Roles in Society" (unpublished Ph.D. diss., North Texas State University, 1952).

22. Damon-Moore, *Magazines for the Millions*, p. 93.

23. Alice Kessler-Harris, *Out to Work: A History of Wage-Earning Women in America* (Oxford University Press, 1982), chapter 5. Also cited in Damon-Moore, *Magazines for the Millions*, p. 93.

24. Damon-Moore, *Magazines for the Millions*, p. 91.

25. Ibid., p. 95.

26. Bok had waged a protracted battle against suffrage in his pages, so even as the vote seemed unavoidable, he would not directly support it. Instead, he bowed to reader pressure by launching a new column that discussed national, state, and local governments. For a detailed discussion of Bok's battle with suffrage in the *Journal*, see Jennifer Scanlon, *Inarticulate Longings: The Ladies' Home Journal, Gender, and the Promises of Consumer Culture* (New York: Routledge, 1995), pp. 109–34.

27. See Mary Ellen Waller, "Popular Women's Magazines, 1890–1917" (unpublished Ph.D. diss., Columbia University, 1987), pp. 230–2.

28. Garvey, *The Adman in the Parlor*.

29. Ruth Cowan, *More Work for Mother: The Ironies of Household Technology from the Open Hearth to the Microwave* (New York: Basic Books, 1983).

30. Bonnie Fox, "Selling the Mechanized Household: 70 Years of Ads in Ladies Home Journal," *Gender & Society*, vol. 4, no. 1 (March 1990), pp. 33, 37. See also Garvey, *The Adman in the Parlor*.

31. Danae Clark coins the term "commodity lesbianism" in discussing the process by which a group that is "1) identifiable 2) accessible 3) measurable and 4) profitable" is targeted specifically with rhetoric and images for its consumption power. See Clark, "Commodity Lesbianism," *Camera Obscura*, vol. 25 (1991).

32. Scanlon, *Inarticulate Longings*, p. 60.

33. Ibid., p. 80.

34. Ibid., p. 52.

35. Ibid., p. 141.

36. Bonnie Dow, *Prime-Time Feminism: Television, Media Culture, and the Women's Movement since 1970* (Philadelphia: University of Pennsylvania Press, 1996), p. 215.

Index

About the Author

AMY BETH ARONSON is an independent author. She is the co-editor of *The Encyclopedia of Men and Masculinity*, *The Gendered Society: Readings*, and Charlotte Perkins Gilman's *Women and Economics*.

DATE DUE